Letters from Dudley

Assembled and Edited by

Peter Cork

to whom they were written between 1980 and 1994

Martine Avenue Productions, Inc.

LETTERS FROM DUDLEY

Dudley Moore, author

Peter Cork, editor

Copyright © 2006, Martine Avenue Productions. Inc.

First published by

Martine Avenue Productions, Inc.

P.O. Box 221, Fanwood, New Jersey 07023, USA

www.dudleycd.com

Cover design: Word Power Graphic Design

Text design and typesetting: Martine Avenue Productions, Inc.

Library of Congress Control Number: 2006920543

ISBN 0977787400

Published in the United States of America in 2006

INTRODUCTION

Surprisingly, it was Dudley who first said, "Let's be pen-pals!" He had just gone to live in Los Angeles, one of his extraordinary changes in career, where his first two films, *10* and *Arthur*, were to establish him at the very top of the Hollywood world. Why he had chosen me for the wonderful correspondence which followed still leaves me in amazement.

We had been friends for many years and I can only think I reminded him of his roots, which he sometimes felt he had left far behind. Sadly I never kept that first letter with his suggestion we should write regularly, but 44 more were to come, in which he told me of his life and work in Hollywood and expressed a depth of thought which may surprise people who only know his outward and outgoing personality.

After his untimely death, it seems to me that these letters are too precious just to keep to myself and I have decided to make them public. These are Dudley's own words during a fascinating period in his life. Any profits they make will go to the two charities that were close to him – Music For All Seasons, which takes the healing power of live music into many types of institutions, and the Dudley Moore Research Fund for PSP, which is attempting to find a cure for the illness which sadly took him from us.

I first met Dudley Moore when he was only sixteen years of age. I had just become the Music Master at Dagenham County High School in the Autumn of 1950. It was my first post after training at Goldsmiths College, national service in the R.A.F. and a further year at the Royal College of Music to study composition. By this time I really wanted to write film music but a year as a freelance composer proved this impossible. So reluctantly, I returned to music teaching. I could not have known that it would be so enjoyable, or that at the start of my career I would encounter one of the most brilliant pupils I could ever hope to meet.

Dagenham was a most unusual suburban town, known by most people at the time for the Dagenham Girl Pipers, a famous female band. The town had been formed in 1936 as a slum clearance for London's East End and was often held up as an example of how not to create a council housing estate. It spread out over several miles but every street and terraced house was exactly alike, often blocks of four with a half circular arch to divide the central ones and give access to the back passage-way. Even after working in the area for seventeen years, I could still get lost if I moved off my beaten track. This is where Dudley lived, 146 Baron Road, his father working on the railway.

Introduction

Dagenham County High was a coeducational Grammar School and I found it an immensely happy place. There was much musical activity with choirs and orchestras and a House Music and Drama Festival every year, which gave as much importance to the arts as football, cricket and athletics. Dudley was then in his fifth year preparing for his School Certificate, the equivalent now of GCSE. He was already a fine musician and had won a Junior Scholarship to the Guildhall School of Music for Saturday morning tuition as a violinist. (His Mother, a very strong minded woman, had chosen this music academy as it was the nearest one to Dagenham on the tube.) He was also a gifted pianist as I was soon to learn with much pleasure, and he played the organ at a local church.

It is often said that Dudley was unhappy and bullied at school. He was of small stature and had a club foot which caused him much embarrassment, and it is said he learned to defuse this situation by becoming a comic and making people laugh. This may have been the case before I met him, but I can only say that by this time he was surely the most popular boy in the school. He was loved by everybody for his music, his constant humour and his happy personality.

I only have small memories of that Fifth Year Music certificate class and the boys and girls who formed it. We studied Mozart's 40th Symphony in G Minor and years later Dudley used a movement from this as background for one of his first films, *30 is a Dangerous Age, Cynthia.* I recall we also studied some Schubert songs, including the dramatic "Erlking." At 18, Dudley came to one of my parties and gave us an early rendering of his wonderful burlesque, "Die Flabbergast," based on that song. It was amazingly funny and professional, and was to be one of his show-pieces throughout his career.

We worked together for four years, through his Higher Certificate, (now the dreaded A Level) and a scholarship year before Oxford University. Dudley was a brilliant pupil but he often left work until the very last moment, only to produce something completely exceptional. (He was to continue this at University when for his second, B.Mus Degree, he composed his String Quartet, virtually the only thing required, two weeks before the deadline.) There were only a few years between us and I often think Dudley taught me just as much as I taught him.

There was much more to our relationship than master and pupil. We had a fifty-strong choir and Dudley was my wonderful accompanist. His sense of humour was in full flow and there were many moments in rehearsal when Dudley would twinkle at the piano and the whole choir would collapse in uncontrollable mirth. (I would get so angry with him!)

I had lodgings in Seven Kings, with Mrs. Nobbs, a kindly woman who owned an old-fashioned upright piano, all curlicues and candelabra, the sort adored by Liberace. Better still, she had a music chest stocked with Edwardian duets. Dudley and I delighted in playing these piano transcriptions of Beethoven symphonies, as well as "The Maiden's Prayer," and "Flick and Flock, the Fireman's Gallop," the latter entertaining many a school concert.

Even then, Dudley was an exceptional sight reader and could play at sight the most complex Bach Fugue, something way beyond my powers. His prowess as a violinist was his chief public expression of talent and I recall how he was summoned to meet Dame Sybil Thorndike at the nearby Kingsley Hall, a Community Centre where we often performed our school concerts. (Mahatma Gandhi had stayed there in the Thirties.) Leonard Marchant, a flutist, together with Dudley, went before this rather formidable actress. But like so many ladies to come, she was very smitten with his musicality and persona. Dudley was a tower of strength in the school orchestra and I remember composing a piece for him, rather too similar to Walton's Violin Concerto. Sadly I never heard Dudley's first composition, "Anxiety", a piece he often later referred to fondly, for he had written it when he was twelve.

The years went by and Dudley passed Higher Schools with flying colours, became Deputy Head Boy and was a hero and friend to all. (Norma Winstone, now the celebrated jazz singer, tells how as a first year student, she would creep into the Hall during the lunch hour and hide behind a pillar to hear him play the piano.)

In his Scholarship year there was a struggle between the demands on his time. Could he continue his work

Introduction

as Choir accompanist and also take one of the leads in the school play, *She Stoops to Conquer?* That was before he went to Magdalen College, Oxford, to audition for an Organ Scholarship. He had to use an extra contraption he fitted on his shoe in order to reach the pedals with his left club foot. He had not succeeded in a similar audition at Cambridge, so was in a relaxed mood, not expecting to achieve anything here. But the fates were with him and he was awarded the scholarship. When his Mother was given the news she is said to have run into the Dagenham street shouting "My son's going to Oxford University!" After that he could do what he liked, continuing with all the music activities and playing Tony Lumpkin in the Oliver Goldsmith play. (I have a fond memory of him standing on a table, tankard in hand, singing a drunken catch.) The school was also given a half day holiday in recognition of Dudley's achievement, the first pupil to reach Oxford or Cambridge. This made him more popular than ever.

It was with some sadness that his Dagenham days came to an end and I think he was nervous about the new environment that awaited him. In the holidays he came to stay at my home in Folkestone and we delighted in our music making together. On a Sunday evening we took a bus to the little village of Elham and went to the service at the church in the village square. Despite being a church organist at Dagenham, Dudley did not have a specific faith, but he was very impressed with the colour, spectacle, theatricality and music in this beautiful building. After this he passed for a time out of my orbit. I went to visit him at Magdalen but remember little of this, other than the echoing corridors around the cloisters. (Dudley said how much he liked to hear the sound of high heels tip-tapping on the flagstones!)

In the Summer of 1958, I had written some organ music for an actor, John Stewart Anderson, who was to give religious monologues in Greyfriars Kirk, during the Edinburgh Festival. Dudley was also to be there and it was a great pleasure to meet up with him and to spend a day together. He seemed happy and relaxed, and after graduation had already established a reputation in cabaret, jazz and composition, not to mention being the pianist in the bands of Vic Lewis and John Dankworth. A mere two years later would come the stupendous show, *Beyond the Fringe.* Dudley's career went into the stratosphere as the show went from the Edinburgh Festival, to London and eventually New York. I caught up with it at the little Fortune Theatre just behind Drury Lane. Dudley's music was an integral part of the show and I have fond memories of his pastiche of Nicholas Brodsky's R.A.F. music from "Way to the Stars" and his version of Peter Pears singing "Little Miss Muffett," his voice suddenly ascending on 'curds away'. He always did have an amazing countertenor!

Some time after *Beyond the Fringe* came to an end, the television years with Peter Cook began. (How often my name has been mistaken for his!) *Not only, but Also* became a favourite household commodity, especially the Pete and Dud sketches and the final song, "Goodbyeee," with Dudley's high, camp, ultimate scream. (The BBC, for economy, wiped many of these precious tapes for tape stock, which made Dudley very angry.)

After this, they had a new show, *Behind the Fridge*, and I went to see it at the Cambridge Theatre. Dudley loved to ad lib, and to include the names of any friends he knew to be in the audience. I was not surprised to hear a scurrilous anecdote about a Mr. and Mrs. Cork. Afterwards I went backstage and Dudley was his usual self, completely unfazed by fame, always concerned for his guest's well-being. I asked to use his cloakroom for a special reason. Ingrid Bergman had been playing the theatre before Dudley and this had been her dressing-room too. I wanted to boast that I had used the same facilities as the star from *Casablanca*!

Our connection continued over the years. Eventually I became so obsessed with the delights of writing period music that I decided to give up full time teaching and see if I could make a professional living from it. After 27 years as a Grammar School Music teacher, now at the age of fifty, I wanted a new career. But how to get started? There was only one person to ask and of course that was Dudley.

He at once gave me some names to approach and this led eventually to Bruton Music where Robin Phillips, to my amazement, gave me the chance to compose my first period album of 'library music'. My first Album was to be music for the Theatre, from Edwardian days to the Thirties. Working for firms such as Chappells, Essex and Studio G, I was to make five more, comprising over a hundred numbers. I scored for everything from Full Orchestra to Military Band, Dance Band to Chamber Group and Piano, covering such topics as the Victorian Era, popular song in the Thirties and Forties, Jazz and the Big Band Sound and the Golden Age of Hollywood, the latter taking me back to the dream of my student days

All this had certainly begun with Dudley's help and advice. In that second part of my life and in a completely new career, our positions as master and pupil were now absolutely reversed. For this I will always be utterly grateful.

And it was about this time that our long and fascinating correspondence was to begin.

[Editor's Note: I will of necessity be adding my explanatory sentences, paragraphs or longer sequences, in all that follows. I will always do this in brackets.]

Introduction

PUBLISHER'S NOTE

Martine Avenue Productions thanks Peter Cork for having kept Dudley's letters safe all these years, and for his hard work in assembling, editing and preparing this volume for publication.

These letters are exactly as written, with the following exceptions: the editor has removed certain personal comments relating to his own work and life; he has also removed personal information that would be an invasion of privacy, including addresses and phone numbers.

It is important to note that Dudley's letters have both American and British spellings, as was his habit. Dudley's punctuation and wording have not been changed. He often used three dots to reflect a pause in the thought. This does not in any instance indicate that text has been removed.

Dudley's original letters were typed by his secretary. Dudley reviewed the letters carefully, and wrote in many notes by hand, as well as adding to or changing the punctuation. All of Dudley's changes are included in this text. His signatures and hand-written postscripts are also included, although the postscripts are reduced in size by 30 per cent to fit on the printed page. Finally, for clarity, all film and show titles have been printed in italics.

May 3, 1980.

Dear Peter,

I was delighted to hear from you and to get both your letter and the Christmas letter that you sent to your Australian friends.

I'm pleased things seem to be moving along, especially in the important area of the Essex Music connection. I make it sound as romantic as *The French Connection* but you know what I mean! It's a connection that I think can generate a fair amount of income because of the repetition value. 'Repetition value' sounds almost too American, doesn't it! Rest assured I haven't suddenly found myself to be a native Californian, although I don't feel particularly English either.

Living out here is very much to my taste because I have a lot of really good friends here and as you know, the work could not be better for me. I'm glad you enjoyed *10*, and I must tell you that the success I've had from it in many ways has had very little impact on my way of life. I think the only thing it does is give me a bit more money and access to scripts that I would like to do. People here look upon me not as a small-part character-comedian but rather as a leading man either in a comedy or in a straight part. This is very gratifying to me and as you yourself mentioned in your letter, is sort of very surprising considering the way I've been most of my life. Right now I'm feeling better than I ever have, not because of this success, because I think it has become a <u>psychological</u> success, if you like. At last I feel the confidence in myself and an acceptance which is very peaceful for me. I don't have the anxieties I used to have about life and my enjoyment of it. I seem to have a really terrific time these days, and I must say it was hard to see myself ever getting to this point, although I always hoped I would break through to this rather more peaceful plateau. It seems to me the main thing I've learned is that confidence and acceptance of oneself are the most important things in life. Once that basis is achieved, everything else seems to take care of itself. I don't feel smug so much as self assured. My honesty with myself and others is of great relief and it's hard to think why we all put this off until such a late date. I think we all fear the intimacy that honesty implies--closeness is always frightening I suppose.

I was very amused by the cutting you sent me. It's one of the more creative corruptions of my name that I've seen in recent years! *[I had sent Dudley a photograph from the Folkestone newspaper. A local cinema had lost the two last letters of his name and the notice-board stated, '10' starring Dudley Moo!]* I'm so delighted that you enjoyed my performance in this film. I think it's the first performance that I have given where I am basically being myself, whatever that means. It's the first time I've allowed myself not to assume a caricature voice or whatever, and this has happened because of my ability to accept myself and let that be seen in my <u>work</u> as well.

If and when I get to London, which is very much in the air at the moment, I would certainly love to see you and catch up with you and your news. Rest assured if I come this time, I will give you a buzz on the telephone. Although I'm only going to be staying a couple of days to see my Mother and sister before I launch into the next year with three films back to back! I start a film in June called *Arthur*, one probably in October called *Dangerously*, and then one in the New Year, (a straight part) called *Six Weeks*. I have another four films which I'm very interested in doing after that, including a film version of *Biggles*! However I haven't committed to any of these because I don't know what I really want to do in a year's time and I want to keep my options open for a bit.

In answer to your question, I did escape most of the floods and hurricanes that swept California recently. Luckily I have about two hundred yards of beach in front of me plus a breakwater which keeps the heavy surf away. People in Malibu with a very narrow beach frontage were less lucky and as you know there were a lot of really awful disasters. Californian houses are not built for rain and I did have my share of leakage although not as bad as two or three years ago when the skylight broke and rain flooded in for days. I was in Australia and Tuesday *[Tuesday Weld, his wife at the time]* went crackers trying to get someone to repair the skylight and couldn't-- since every available man was employed elsewhere, so she spent her life emptying buckets and wasn't very pleased about that!

You said something very interesting -- that "life seems to unfold in chapters, like a Victorian novel, and utter finality once a particular chapter is closed." I think this is only to a certain extent true and depends on how much importance you give to your own choice of what you do in your life. There is obviously a restricted area in which we live our lives. I don't mean from an environmental point of view but from a view that is determined by our early life, our aptitudes, our genes, etc. I think that within that more or less restricted sphere, we have great choice and can make our life what we want except for the contingencies of life that we are cursed with a lot of the time. I believe very much that we choose for ourselves what we want in our lives and <u>that</u> is the inspiring and poetic thing about life as far as I'm concerned.

Hope to see you soon if I can get back to London. Thanks again for writing at great length and I'm glad that you did write on a personal note. After all, what else could you write on!

All the best from

October 17, 1980

Dear Peter,

Many thanks for your last letter. I wanted to address myself to a couple of points that you made. I think sometimes that a feeling of being reincarnated can be an intense longing for another sort of life where things are as we want them to be. Maybe the someone else you felt you were at the moment you made this jump was in fact the you that has been lurking inside yourself all these years. This may sound as fanciful a psychological theory as the reincarnation theory, but it seems to me to make sense in the context of what I am trying to achieve in my life. I think it is interesting that psychologically we are often incapable of accepting a large part of ourselves. We repress it and are scarcely aware of it to the point that we only notice the anxious fumes this dark being exhales in our minds! I suppose I prefer to believe that what I am now is everything I am and will be, that there is no future and past that is worth considering, that the present is what we have and should cherish. I know that it is very difficult to hang onto the present and live in its terms, but I try to, even though fear keeps me away from that goal all the time.

[I had mentioned reincarnation in my previous letter. I spoke of a strange phenomenon when at very rare occasions of tiredness or extreme emotion, for the tiniest fraction of time, I seemed to become another person with a completely different history. I don't think I agreed with Dudley's interesting analysis of this!]

The other point you made which fascinated me was about having a mission in life to do certain things. I feel that we all have a <u>desire</u> to do certain things, but once the word mission or obligation comes into it, my enjoyment of my work diminishes. I'm basically a total hedonist and proud of it! I only want to do what gives me pleasure since I think that's the only way I can give pleasure to other people. The fact that I give other people pleasure with my own enjoyment is purely incidental. I would never feel that I had to put other people's pleasure before mine, although old patterns sometimes make me fall into that trap.

By the time you get this letter, I hope that I may have talked to you since I'm going to be in England for a few days. The chances of our meeting are sort of slim since I'm there for such a short time, but I will give you a ring and chat at least for a while. (PS. I tried you in Folkestone but missed you. Spoke to your mother.)

I'm writing this in my hotel room in New York where I've just finished filming *Arthur* and I'm looking forward to another holiday in England and then back to Los Angeles. I know from your letter that things are not smooth in England and that your work is not necessarily the fastest way to make a buck, but I'm glad to hear that it is enjoyable because that is of course all any of us needs in our life.

I take your point about people not being able to choose their lives in certain environments and I didn't mean to infer from my previous remarks that this wasn't the case. I think given a fair degree of luck in where one is born and when and to which parents, one is able to choose a life for oneself. Certainly I can't imagine being born in one of the Eastern countries. Their life must be hell and ambition must be down to getting a bowl of rice each week.

On that exhilarating note I will close and hope that I will have seen you in England by the time you get this. If not, we will talk anon. I wish you all the best.

[In 1945, as part of the music course at Goldsmiths College, I wrote a long dissertation on film music. Despite wartime I contacted Hollywood and among others, received two personal, hand-written letters from Roy Webb, Music Director for RKO Radio Pictures. He scored many, many films including my favourite, 'The Enchanted Cottage'. I wondered if he was still alive for I wanted to thank him for his kindness in writing in such detail to a young stranger in another country.]

October 21, 1981

Dear Peter,

It was really nice to hear from you. We haven't been in touch for some time but I guess from my end things really haven't changed too much, except that they are <u>moving</u> a little, which is a relief, after a great deal of delay. I'm starting my first film which is laughingly known as a 'dramatic' piece, *['Six Weeks']* around the middle of November, and then another film, a comedy, where I play a psychoanalyst, *['Lovesick']* around February the 15th, and a third film, if I'm still alive, sometime in June! The films have sort of got backed-up because of strikes and the usual problems and procrastinations associated with film production. I am not used to this, even though I've been here for some time, and I hate the whole process of trying to get so many different strands pulled together for one concerted effort. Hopefully, *Arthur,* my newest film, will come out a week before Christmas in England. It has enjoyed an enormous success here in the States and I hope will have the same effect in Europe. It opened in Sweden very successfully, and I would be particularly gratified if it went well in England.

Everything sounded very active at your end. I was glad to see that you have done so much recording work, and that some very prestigious performers have been associated with your work.

From the musical point of view, I have had a certain amount of activity. I did "Rhapsody in Blue" with the Los Angeles Philharmonic earlier in the Summer and also played three quarters of an hour of Gershwin tunes with a trio (piano, bass and drums). I'm doing a concert on January 3rd with my friend Robert Mann, of the Juilliard String Quartet, and a clarinettist who will join us for a couple of works in the programme. We are doing the Beethoven Violin Sonata in G Major, Opus 30 Number 3, the Mozart Sonata in C Major, K296, Delius' Third Violin Sonata, and two works in which we'll be joined by clarinet, "Contrasts" by Bartok and the Adagio from "Kammerkonzert" by Berg. I think it will be a fun evening although I'm not sure how much of a habit I'm going to make out of concertising. I'm also supposed to be writing a score for the next film I'm doing, *Six Weeks,* which I hopefully will do if I have time --the only problem is that I go straight into the second film, *Valium,* after the first!

I will try and track down Roy Webb for you. I'll see if my agent here can get hold of him. If anybody can, he can. If Roy Webb is alive, I will certainly give you the details of where he is, and probably phone him and alert him of your desire to make contact again. I remember the film, *The Enchanted Cottage,* which haunted me a great deal, mainly because of the horrific aspects of Robert Young's make-up! I seem to remember the music was really rather terrific too. I must try and get hold of that score since it was a very strange film that made a great impression on me.

Sorry to hear about your Mother's accident. My Mother is now eighty, having just turned eighty this June or July. (I can't remember which right now-- although I did at the time, I'm glad to say!) I wanted to come to England to be with her on that birthday, but I was unable to come across. She seems to be reasonably OK, but her breathing is not marvellous. She has to use some sort of medication six times a day which helps her breathe more easily, but tends to slow her down. I must say that if there comes a time when I'm going to be in a great deal of pain and at the mercy of a great deal of inconvenience because of my physical condition, I will certainly feel quite happy about popping a nice friendly lot of medication down my throat. I don't feel morbid about suicide, I just feel it would be a practical end to a lot of horrendous waiting around in agony.

My Mother still lives in Dagenham. She has never wanted to leave. Her friends seem to be there, although most of them are dying off now, and she speaks with great nostalgia of the friends that she's had who have moved away from where she is. She keeps very rare contact with them, even though she has a phone where she is, and could pick it up and talk. I don't know what it is, but I think there is something about her that secretly rather enjoys her insularity, although she is sort of ambivalent about it, sometimes saying she enjoys her privacy, and then saying she feels quite isolated.

I'm going to close now, and watch some television, or something equally decadent. So, I'll talk to you anon.

All the best meanwhile. It was lovely to hear from you again.

PS. I was able to contact Roy Webb's wife. He is in his early nineties now and is apparently an invalid. He is deteriorating rather badly so is unable to correspond with anybody or to talk. I feel that his wife is presently protecting him from all sources outside the house. I felt when I was talking to her that it wasn't the time to ask for an address to write to. However, if you want to write to him, I'm sure the letter would get to him if you sent it either to me or to ASCAP.

[I did write to Roy Webb to thank him, but did not get, or expect to get, a reply. I often wonder if he received my letter. I do hope so.]

[The following was a sad letter but no surprise. I had seen pictures in the press of Dudley and his sister Barbara at his Mother's funeral.]

November 15, 1981

Dear Peter,

I just received your second letter of the 23rd of October, and I wanted to answer it immediately. I had written a letter to you some time ago, but due to changing circumstances, I found myself altering the letter as I went along. I'm enclosing it now, *[Dudley's letter of October 21st,]* so that you can read it, even though it is out of date, especially with the situation regarding my Mother, who died a few weeks ago. I felt rather than altering everything again, I would send you this covering letter, with the original letter that I was going to send in the first place.

I was in town briefly for a television show for London Weekend Television, which coincided rather ironically with my Mother's death. I must say her timing was superb to the end. Don't worry, she would enjoy that sort of joke! It was a very strange thing to experience and I'm very shocked by it, much to my surprise. I seem to be in a situation where I cannot accept or comprehend her death, but that will probably change and soften over the years.

I will not be in London for the premiere of *Arthur* as I'm starting a film in a few days' time which will go through the New Year. However, if I get back, I will be in touch although I have rather a lot of work to do in the coming months. I have added even a fourth film to my agenda! It is called *Unfaithfully Yours*, and is a remake of an old Preston Sturgess (?) film of some years ago. Perhaps you remember it.

I'm going to finish this now, and get it off in the post before I dawdle on altering letters to you until the end of time. Best wishes to you, and thanks again for writing. I'm very pleased that things are pushing ahead for you musically. That is wonderful news. All the best from

December 24, 1981

Dear Peter,

I'm just reading your letter, and am prompted to make a quick reply to a couple of things that you mentioned, with regard to your recording session. I used to record at the Olympic Studios in Barnes all the time, and Keith Grant did some terrific work for me. So I was very pleased that you had been able to use his expertise. I was amused to read that you had used Lennie Bush on drums, because Lennie Bush is a bass player, unless of course, by some miracle, he has suddenly become a

13

very efficient drummer! I've worked with Lennie on a number of occasions, and he is excellent.

[This was my 'Library' Album on Jazz and the Big Band Sound of the Thirties and Forties. I had obviously mistaken the name of the Drummer!]

Isn't it a thrilling experience hearing your arrangement back in a terrific studio, on a multi-track recording? I was always excited and surprised at the sound. There were always things that I hadn't anticipated in my arrangement, that sounded different—generally, things came off better than I expected. Some things came out rather lamely, but on the whole, the thrill of the newness of the sound was just incredible. I smiled when you wrote that you didn't always give the brass enough breathing space. I remember in a piece of mine, giving the trombones a fast move from a low B flat to a B natural, which of course involves a fast move from no extension to a full extension, or the other way around, I can't remember which—which of course is one of my problems! I'm looking forward to getting your tape. I'll be really excited to hear the results of the session. In answer to your enquiry, of course I don't mind. I'm only too delighted to listen to what you have been up to in the last years!

Yes, I believe you are right, that *Unfaithfully Yours* starred Rex Harrison. I'm not sure about Linda Darnell but I'm sure you are right. Hope you enjoy *Arthur*, if and when you see it. It's really quite a funny film, I think, and there's a great spirit about it.

Letters from Dudley

You are correct, that *10* was not that greatly reviewed in England when it first came out, but it is making its third tour around the circuits. The reviews have become increasingly more positive, which is interesting, after a sort of snotty start. This, of course, is very gratifying to me.

For the Gershwin concert, I had to do quite a lot of practising. There were a few passages in the "Rhapsody" *[Rhapsody in Blue]* that were quite tricky. Not exactly from a fingering point of view, but from the point of view of finding out where you were on the piano, especially towards the end, where he starts the sort of train locomotion bit. I seem to do a fairly minimum amount of practice, with generally good results, but I'm trying to keep up a regular stint for the concert in January, since I don't really want to make a fool of myself, at such a potentially critical occasion.

Your suggestion about sending me an "English point of view" is very welcome, but don't feel obligated! I would hate to feel that you were having to deliver a weekly newsletter. I generally keep up with the news here, even though it's not from an English point of view, but that is something I will leave to you and not something I would like to feel is to be thought of as a regular item!

Christmas is now only 48 hours away, so I have a feeling I have to stop and attend to the anxieties of a festival that I'm not too keen on these days. I no doubt will talk to you by way of a letter very soon. All the best for Christmas and the New Year.

I'm not sending any cards this year. I've just not been able to get to it, but you may get a Happy Un-Christmas card from me later on!

All the best from

January 19, 1982

Dear Peter,

Just received your music cassette through the post and I'm sitting and reading your letter, so I am answering as I go along. I have yet to hear the cassette, as I have only just got up from a night of filming, and have to get myself organized for the day, but I will probably listen to it later on this afternoon and tell you my reactions.

Thanks for sending me the reviews of *Arthur* from the English Press. I have seen them, because I have a Durrant's press cutting service that supplies me with the English newspaper material, but thank you very much indeed for the thought. I obviously am disappointed at the reaction in the Press, which has been in many ways quite vindictive towards me, and personally slanted. I agree with you-- I do feel that the Press has got it in for me. I was discussing it with a friend this morning and it's as if I have rejected England, abandoned my family, and am now being punished for it. Curiously enough, I met two English women in the last couple of days who were both quite hostile toward me in a way that I hadn't seen before-- possibly because I was having a good time with a lot of American friends. So I think there is a definite feeling there, and I am prepared for it now, after having seen it in my own mind, and also talked it over with these friends. I'm answering two or three of the critics who have made personal attacks on me, because I don't see why they should get away with that. I don't mind if they don't like a film, but I think that personal attacks are out of order, or at least they will be responded to by me. If I ever see these people I will kick them very hard or put a pie firmly on the nose! However the good news is that *Arthur* has been an unqualified success in Britain, according to the "Daily Variety" that comes out here. I spoke to my brother-in-law earlier today, and he told me that friends of his have seen it more than once already. This is a pattern that happened in America -- where we had wonderful reviews as a matter of fact-- but business was slow at first. Now the film is in its sixth month, or something like that, and has made $80 million, which isn't bad. People have seen it over and over again here, and it's a very popular and, I think, appealing film. But the sort of criticism that has been levelled at it has been like a grand aunt reprimanding a small boy who has kicked the cat, and I really feel angry about some of the remarks. However, it seems to be appealing to the public all over the world and so I have really nothing to complain about. It's just the feeling of being rapped over the knuckles for going away from the English playpen. As you say a little further down in your letter, the public is responding well to it, and for this I am grateful. So stuff the critics!

My concert in New York was indeed a great success, despite one luke-warm but not unkind review in the New York Times. This was predictable. My fellow musicians said we would find no insights in this column, and we didn't. But from musicians whom we all respect, the remarks were positive and delighted, so I feel a great stepping-stone has been crossed, since I was really very fearful of doing a programme where people might know what note I should be playing next! I hope I will do more of it now that I've seen that it is not that much of an ordeal anymore. I enjoyed it, and had a wonderful, loving experience with these dear friends of mine. And in return I will send you copies of the concert. I realise that I have your tapes that just came through, so perhaps we can exchange cassettes as we toddle down life's weary way!

Glad you caught the *(television)* show on Boxing Day evening. I have yet to receive a cassette of the show, but I'm looking forward to seeing what I did. I'm glad the Beethoven pastiche stood up. I do find it quite easy to slip in and out of improvised material to set pieces. I guess I've done it so long now, that it doesn't seem to be anything too remarkable.

As you remark re your weather, it seems to be quite catastrophic everywhere except in California where we have been experiencing really lovely sunshine. Places have been getting something like twenty inches of snow in the rest of the country, and it doesn't seem as though it is going to let up. I believe it is a cyclical action that happens in the weather, as you remarked. I hope it's not the beginning of the end!

Well, I will hope to hear your cassette later on today, and add something to this letter. In the meantime, thanks again for writing, and I will hope to talk to you soon, one way or the other. All the best for the New Year-- and everything else.

Warmest regards from

P.S. Just listened to your cassettes and thought they were really terrific, beautifully recorded--and I spent a very enjoyable time getting very nostalgic. I think my favorite piece of all was the Cockney tune in the 1920 – 1940 selection. It had that marvellous "have a banana" sauce, great charm and humour and a very interesting, unexpected middle section which I really loved. Of course the songs in the Musical Theatre section, like the waltzes, "Gold and Amber" and "Darling Gertie" were particularly enjoyable for me. I loved the piano solos too, especially. They were a nice contrast and the orchestrations were always interesting and varied. Great stuff Peter, very enjoyable. Thank you for sending it to me.

[This was the Bruton Library Album on theatrical music, from Edwardian days to the Thirties. I played and recorded the piano solos myself but found it such a nerve-racking experience, I never did this again. On all future Albums I allowed the session pianist to play the piano numbers.]

March 15, 1982

Dear Peter,

Many thanks for your letter. I am delighted that you enjoyed the concert tapes. I must say that I am very proud of myself for having had the nerve to get up there and play! I have been promising myself to do this for a long time, but never really had the guts to do so. By the way I don't think you were dim-witted in the Dagenham days. I just don't think that whatever talent I had was particularly elegantly formed. It was in a sort of blustering, non-self-confident shapeless mass which was hard to pin down. I think all that has happened in recent years is that I've worked a little more consistently, and less anxiously, and have been able to tie a few of the frayed strings together through a touch more discipline. *[I had called myself dim-witted for not fully recognising Dudley's talents at the time!]*

As you said, the Bartok is quite difficult. Not, of course, for the piano, but certainly for the clarinet and violin however. I did find a few places a little tricky, especially a couple where the time signature was hard to make work in a natural way. For instance, the alternating 4/4 5/8 section in the last movement defied my efforts to make it lilt, until the rhythm had eased into my bones a little bit.

I'm glad you enjoyed *Arthur* so much. I'm tickled pink that it is doing so well in England, despite some fairly 'superior' reviews at times in the Press. As you say, it may well be sour grapes on the part of some critics, who feel that I am abandoning ship by going to other climes.

The filming of *Lovesick*, which used to be known as *Valium!*, is proceeding very easily and with much enjoyment. I find the people that I'm working with very congenial, and am having the best of times. It's also one of the busiest, which is why this letter will be rather short, but I wanted to get this off to you and thank you for your rather longer, and rather more interesting letter. So until the next time, all the best from me.

Letters from Dudley

[The following letter came just after the Falklands War.]

September 8, 1982

Dear Peter,

Many thanks for your letter. Just to reassure you that I did receive your album, 'The Danceband Years'. Unfortunately, I have not had a chance to listen to it yet. I have been so pressed for time. We have been filming very hard for the past months, and I have scarcely had time to take a breath. The hours are so long, from about 6 am to 8 pm, including getting up and getting home. Consequently, I have been unable to relax and to do anything very much, but when I do have a little bit of time, I am going to listen to the album!

I can't agree with you more about the rubbish that was purveyed in the English press about the regeneration of England. It was almost obscene to think people would consider the joyous possibility of a 'hat trick' in such a dubious area. Princess Di and the baby, the Falkland Islands and the World Cup. It seems the war has become a 'show biz' item, just like everything else. I find myself increasingly grim as the endless list of deaths and killings and tragedies in the world goes on relentlessly. It does make one think that it might be quite pleasant to leave sometime!

Did I tell you that I saw the film *Laura* again? The theme was used endlessly, both as scored music and as source music, appearing in the background, obviously emanating from a cafe orchestra, or a radio, or whatever. Of course the magic of the film had, to a large extent, worn off, and even the haunted quality of the theme seemed to have lessened over the years. Somehow it all seemed different seeing it on the television screen. The first time that I saw it in a movie house must have impressed me enormously, but that fantasy has faded a little bit now. How sad!

I am including a cassette of the music that I wrote for the film with Mary Tyler Moore called *Six Weeks*. The theme is very simple, as you can tell. In fact, when I first improvised it as a temporary track for the film editors, I was rather embarrassed. It was such a simple theme over the old stand-by of a cycle of fifths. However, I have used it, since somehow the theme has gotten emblazoned on my mind, and the result is on the tape with various harmonisations and moods. There is a secondary theme which you will hear much more of, a blatantly romantic Rachmaninoff-type theme.

Also included are some jazz bits and pieces which we used for source music at party sequences and so forth. You don't have to take too much notice!

Thanks again for writing and I hope to listen to your record as soon as I can. Sorry not to have done so beforehand. I hope things are well with you.

All the best from

[The cassette he sent me was the one with Dudley's recording and treatment of his theme from 'Six Weeks', one of the best things he ever composed. It included a myriad of variations and became one of the most precious things Dudley ever sent me. I loaned it to a production company making a television programme about Dudley's music. Sadly it was stolen in a burglary. It played for over thirty minutes and was quite priceless, for I doubt that any other copy exists.]

✥

November 19, 1982

Dear Peter,

I am answering your letter quickly before I run off to Miami for an award ceremony I'm rather pleased about, since it is emanating from the National Association of Theatre Owners in the United States. They have named me 'Male Box-office Star of the Year,' which is of some significance in the sense that it means I have attained some sort of commercial clout in the industry! So it is a useful item to be associated with. After all the potential silliness of that, Susan and I are going off to Fort Lauderdale for a few days to have a small rest before I start off on the next film.

[Dudley's close companion at the time was Susan Anton. She was taller than Dudley and the Press delighted in showing pictures of them together.]

After that, we are back here for Thanksgiving although, as an Englishman, I'm not sure that I am really giving thanks for anything—and then only too soon, off to Christmas. I have a lot of activity between now and Christmas since the film *Six Weeks* is opening in Los Angeles and New York during that period, and I'm going to be in both places for those premieres. I also have a lot of publicity to do for them, talking to endless journalists. There is a process by which I sit in a hotel suite for about four hours with a television camera and each journalist has a tape put in the video machine with which he departs at the end of the interview. It is somewhat gruelling since one is tending to go over the same ground time and time again, but it is quite good fun.

Glad you were able to hear the music that I wrote. *[This was the 'Six Weeks' cassette.]* I do orchestrate it myself, although I generally do it in a short score form, and indicate the exact movement of the instruments, leaving it to somebody who is termed 'an orchestrator', (rather loosely of course), to write out the thing on a <u>long</u> score. This certainly saves an enormous amount of time, as you can well imagine from your orchestration feats. We may at some time be releasing a version of the main theme, with a slight alteration of the middle part, but it rather depends on how the film goes. Everybody is very cautious in the record industry here, since there is so much pirating these days, it is not always worth putting something out.

Just in passing, curiously I saw Dana Andrews in Elaine's restaurant in New York about a week or so ago. He looked in pretty good shape, I must say. If he had a drinking problem, it certainly wasn't showing that night. He looked very grey, and this seemed to change him a great deal, but his face is very much the same. Certainly not ravaged by anything too much or important, it seems. *[I had mentioned Dana Andrews and this press comment, when speaking of the film 'Laura', his fine performance in it and David Racksin's glorious theme tune.]*

Thanks for the newspaper clipping, which I was interested to read. I can't agree with the writer about me having to 'resort' to the coarseness of a drunk because of teenage expectations. Steve Gordon, the writer, just wrote the script the way he wanted, not I think with any commercial end in view because, apart from anything, it is impossible to know what works anyway! There's no formula. If there were, my God, we'd all be much happier about the prospects of what we did. After all, *Arthur* is about a man who is a drunk almost permanently, and that in itself does not mean that you are going to have a commercial film, merely

26

because you are going to have a drunk on screen. Also in regard to that article, I certainly did do a drama after that, *['Six Weeks']* but have since done two comedies, and I'm about to do another one! I don't think one drama in six films is showing too much of a switch! However, I'm drawn to the idea of doing drama...not because of any commercial consideration, which has never been in my mind anyway, but merely because I find that the expression of myself can be fuller and more relaxed in a dramatic piece. I don't want to do anything that is violent or anything that is morbid or whatever. I just want to do things that are, I suppose, celebrating the joy that we can get out of life, if I may put it in a rather clumsily 'poetic' fashion!

Well, somewhere during this letter I dashed out to get my dry cleaning and take some video cassettes back to the rental place, just to show what a regular, ordinary, unspoiled person I am! I will send you five pounds if you can guess where else I went in this letter!

Will have to stop now... I'm trying to catch up with the essential mail before I leap off to the glamour of Miami. It was really nice to hear from you again, Peter, and I'll talk to you later, no doubt.

All the best as usual from

March 4, 1983

Dear Peter,

Just got your cassette tape which I will, as you suggest, take in the car with me for an outing, on my way to the studio tomorrow morning. I'm looking forward to hearing all the good work that you've done! You certainly seem to have a lot of things brewing or up your sleeve. I hope that they will come through for you. I am about six to seven weeks away from the end of a really horrendous schedule and I'm looking forward to a break which I'm sure I've talked to you about before. I am, as you said, working on *Unfaithfully Yours*. In fact, you might have already got a letter in which I discussed that film and others that I have recently done. The Bulldog Drummond type project was either *Dangerously* or *Biggles*. I can't remember which I identified in that category. In any case, I turned down *Biggles* because I thought it was a very monochromatic character and the other, *Dangerously*, sort of slid away into the sea like houses on the Californian shoreline because of a budget that was too inflated. I was sort of grateful in the end since there were a lot of problems surrounding the project. Not least about fifteen different opinions as to how the thing should go from the story point of view.

I haven't seen Peter Cook for some time. I'm obviously aware of him looking a little older, having caught up with him probably more in these last years than you have. He became heavily grey quite prematurely and has certainly put on a lot of weight (over the last few years). I am sort of fascinated to see his new film, *Yellowbeard* which I have a feeling will be a bit of a hodge-podge of styles. I can't say that I miss our time together. I know in many ways that I'm an isolated person and enjoy this isolation so that friends drift in and out of my life and I'm not always aware of their coming and going. It sounds callous but it's not meant to be. It's just the fact that I learned this particular way of life in my early years.

As you mentioned in your letter, it is certainly shocking to realise that Steve Gordon died at the age of 44. *[He was the script writer for 'Arthur'.]* It makes you think...or does it? I don't know. I can't say that I'm any more careful about the way that I live. I think that Steve was a particularly hyper-anxious type and, rather sinisterly, his family all seemed to die at an early age. He had one surviving brother, I believe. His parents died at about the same age of 44.

I'm off to bed now. It's 10.15 pm, and I have to get up early to get to the studio, so I will stop dribbling on for the moment, and as I say--I look forward to listening to the tape in the morning.

As always,

Letters from Dudley

May 17, 1983

Dear Peter,

Couldn't agree with you more about your assessment of the film, *Lovesick*. Once my character got together with the girl, the story indeed seemed over. In the original version there was much more jeopardy involved in my leaving the psychoanalytic society in New York, but the way the film turned out it was too bland. I think also that the critics were a little hard on me sometimes and that Barry Norman was right about it being sort of an unforgivable sin to leave England. My film *Six Weeks* was in fact made before *Lovesick* and should come out at some point but I'm not sure when. I feel it's my best work to date. A very simple, poetic, joyful film despite a very sad touching story.

I enjoyed your record enormously. I listened to it the day I got it. In fact, I have a feeling that I wrote a letter right afterwards, but I'm so behind on correspondence that I sometimes am a little muddled as to what I've answered and what I haven't. But notwithstanding this, I did enjoy the tape with all of its variety of styles which I thought were so wonderfully accurate. In connection with all this, I trust that there are more doors opening in the world you're now occupying musically. I just talked to my friend Chris Karan who is a drummer I work with when I'm in England and he said that the musical scene generally was very depressed and there was not really too much going on because of lack of money and perhaps lack of incentive.

Thank you for mentioning the Oscar ceremony. I'm glad that at least my composure was noteworthy! My music was nominated for 'Best Score', not by the Academy which awards the Oscars, but by the Hollywood Foreign Press which awards Golden Globes. I must that say I share your feelings about Spielberg et al. It does seem really stupid when you have to choose between *E.T.*, *Gandhi*, and *Tootsie*. Funny to hear you make a remark about Jane Russell! I must say that she does seem to have got harder over the years. Not the sort of person I'd like to have breakfast with. Cornell Wilde was rather touching I thought. Perhaps I feel that because he sat down beside me and expressed great admiration to me. How strange it is to have somebody who had blood dripping from the keyboard in "Chopin's Biography" come up to me and say how much he admired <u>my</u> work! *[This was the biographical film 'A Song to Remember'.]* Similarly Gene Kelly did it fairly recently. I was starting to say how much I adored him in all of his films and he said "I don't want to talk about me, I want to talk about you." It's so odd to have the idols of one's past now becoming fans of mine. Very strange, but... what the heck!

I was interested in what you had to say about being born under lucky stars. I tend not to believe in luck--which may be lucky for me! I do feel that it is desire which motivates one's life and my desire has been to find myself. Perhaps the greatest reward has been, apart from a gigantic feeling of personal insight and acceptance, a certain amount of professional success. I'm not sure about the business of being in the right place at the right time. So many places are 'right' and one can <u>make</u> them the right time if one chooses. Hope this doesn't sound too smug... it's not meant to be, but I feel if one feels that luck is a factor then there could be a self-fulfilling prophecy of failure in the offing. It seems to create an 'if only' situation which to me is a non-acceptance of the present and a mere yearning for the future. I think one of the crucial things is how we deal with that awful unfinished business of our parents. It is central...a life and death struggle to cut loose from the umbilical cords that tend to strangle us unless we can observe them with charity and accept that we'll always have it around our necks! My metaphors are getting unintentionally gory, but it's a gory business, isn't it!? I think that knowing and observing who I am has been the greatest factor in my life and has contributed to every success that I've had in ways that it is difficult to appreciate.

Anyway, enough of this stuff. Although I think it is totally central to our lives, I don't want to press it too much when the effect may be a little on the boring side for somebody else. I cannot help being a little evangelistic about the exploration within, since it has freed me in many ways. Discoveries of my past continue. Discoveries of relentless patterns repeating themselves over and over again seem to come thick and fast, and I learn and observe and stop criticising myself now, so that I can accept the spots that this leopard has got!

I may or may not be coming to England sometime within the next six months since I may have some time off. If I do, I'll be in touch. I have a feeling I've said that before, but you must excuse the repetition in my letters. It comes with the passing years!

All the best as usual, and thanks again for writing.

Yours,

June 23, 1983

Dear Peter,

Just received your letter the other day, and am answering it immediately. Sorry you missed *Six Weeks*, but perhaps it will come out on TV in a while. I think it will also appear on video tape at some point. I'm not surprised that the critics were unkind to it. It seems to be a way of life with regards to this film. It has been rather painful for me to read all this stuff anymore, to the point that I have cancelled the press-cuttings service that I've had for many years now in England, so that I don't give myself the temptation to read what these people say. I think you are aware of the general climate that surrounds me now. I don't mind, and in fact I'm getting to the point where I don't really care. I feel secure enough in what I'm doing not to be disheartened by it. (!) It may well just be a phase that goes on forever. If so, it doesn't matter either, because I know that I will always work.

It is curious that you asked me if I was on nodding acquaintance with various, people since one of them that you mentioned I met only recently... Alice Faye. She was at a party-- the 80th birthday party in fact for Wilfred Hyde-White. I played the piano in the bar at the restaurant where we were having the party for some time and had great fun doling out all those lovely old tunes like: "I Fall In Love Too Easily," "Laura," "The Boy Next Door," "Long Ago And Far Away," and so forth. Alice Faye introduced herself and that was a great surprise and delight I must say. I've met Fred Astaire very briefly. Jimmy Stewart I met recently and Henry Fonda just before he died, although I didn't get to say much to him.   Again, Bette Davis I have just been introduced to but can't say that I have held her either in conversation or in any other capacity! I seem to have garnered unlikely admirers in Hollywood.   Unlikely, because who would have thought that Burt Lancaster and Kirk Douglas would admire my work tremendously!? Or Fred MacMurray and June Haver, Groucho Marx, etc?? It is strange because these figures seem to be, as you quite rightly put it, in some mythological time warp and it is hard to think of them appreciating anything that they haven't done themselves! Believe me, however, I'm not blasé about all of this. The other night I met Frank Sinatra and his wife Barbara, which for me was a quite awesome event. He does seem to be an amazing person and a terrific singer-- and I did find myself more than a mite nervous when I spoke to him! When I finally was able to say how much I have loved him over the years he surprised me by saying that he had been disappointed not to get to my Carnegie Hall concert or the one in L.A. that I did recently with the L.A. Chamber Orchestra when I played the Beethoven Triple Concerto. He thought that was a terrific idea and was expressing great admiration, so it is all very bizarre, isn't it?

I was delighted to hear that your royalties from BBC and ITV came to a good 'whack'! That is good news! I think that is the marvellous thing about royalties. They seem to germinate secretly in a dark place, and then come through the letterbox with a resounding message of joy and good will! I think that sort of royalty, with a bit of luck and, hopefully, longevity of the material, will continue for many years. It's like having non-risky investments up one's sleeve.

Couldn't agree with you more on Mrs. Thatcher. What an appallingly strange and constipated old bat she is! I agree with you entirely. Her stubbornness is really, in my view, quite dangerous.

Yes, I do believe that Dorothy McGuire and Robert Young are still alive. I know Robert Young is, since he has a serial here I think called 'General Hospital.' I think you would be rather appalled to see it, as I think I was when I first laid eyes on it. I thought "How could the man from 'The Enchanted Cottage' betray us like this, and get into some soapy serial like that?" It was strange to see him turned into this benign doctor. I'd always thought of him in that film and it's curious, I guess, that I fall into the same trap, naturally enough, as everybody else and view an actor in the light in which I first saw him! People, still, in England perhaps see me as part of 'Dud and Pete', whereas, in fact, I've become something which is not different but perhaps a development of that. Everybody really wants me to just stick where I was! Dorothy McGuire is also alive, I think, and very much the same, curiously. She has a face that seems to have preserved itself rather beautifully.

I see that you have heard of my recital in New York and L.A., where I did, as I think I mentioned before, Beethoven's Triple Concerto with Robert Mann (my friend from the Juilliard String Quartet) and Nathaniel Rosen (who is a particularly brilliant Cellist who studied with Piatigorsky). We played Carnegie Hall and then with the L.A. Chamber Orchestra under Gerard Schwarz. The New York concert was with the St. Paul's Chamber Orchestra of Minnesota, under the direction of Pinchas Zukerman, whom I'm sure you know, is a great violinist. He's a slightly bluff and cavalier musician with whom Robert Mann had many a disagreement. I respect Bob's point of view, I must say, since he, in a sense, is a more serious musician. Although 'Pinky' as he is known to the slightest acquaintance, is a wonderful violinist, he tends to make all music an emotional affair, with the result that the structure of the piece tends to falter a little because of an almost wayward passion of the moment. I would normally agree with this point of view, except that I think it is sometimes perhaps, in his case, taken to excess. I remember seeing Zukerman play in a Brandenburg Concerto at the Aldeburgh Festival many years ago, at a speed that made Benjamin Britten's hair visibly rise on end! I could almost hear him 'tut-tutting' in his box. I must say that I didn't like it either, but one cannot help admiring the gorgeous qualities of Zukerman's playing. The experience in L.A. was more delightful. I'm hoping to get a tape of the concert which was rather primitively done I gather since we didn't have any TV or radio or tape recordings set up. I will try and send you a copy if and when I get it.

A passing note. I see you are back in the Lake District again. That does sound an attractive prospect I must say! Sometimes I do yearn for the green hills and valleys and all that stuff!

Yes, as a youth I was moonstruck over a French girl called Marie-José Porak. I met her again when I was doing 'Beyond the Fringe' and then lost contact. I can't say that I swoon over her name now, but I do feel my heart twinge!

All the best as usual from your pen pal! Hope I'll make it over to England soonish.

All regards as usual,

[Perhaps the most extraordinary thing for me, in Dudley's Hollywood letters, is how he describes the evening when at a party, Alice Faye comes up and introduces herself.

During the war years I lived in the Kentish town of Ashford. The Battle of Britain took place in the skies above us and our railway junction was frequently bombed. As a teenager, I voraciously read the complete works of Dickens, mostly in the air raid shelter. The one touch of colour was our weekly trip to the Cinema where stars such as Betty Grable and Rita Hayworth lightened our days. I particularly loved Grable and Alice Faye in the Fox Technicolor Musicals and they acquired a legendary character. But one never thought of these ladies as real, flesh and blood people. Yet here, many years later, is one of them talking to my erstwhile pupil. Amazing!

It was similar with his introduction to Gene Kelly. I recall how Dudley and I went to the pictures, probably when he stayed in Folkestone, and saw Kelly in a gangster movie.

Dudley was particularly taken with his waif-like co-star, Pier Angeli. Who could have thought then, that way in the future Dudley would enthuse to Gene about 'Singing in the Rain', only to be told, in effect --it's your turn now!]

୧୬

December 8, 1983

Dear Peter,

So glad that you are listening to the Triple Concerto again. You are quite right, I did enjoy especially the Hungarian Rondo episode. I felt that it needed a little bit of more than usual rubato. Some of the orchestra looked almost shocked, pleasantly so I must add, when I pulled the time around so much, but it did seem to demand it. I'm glad that you felt that the movement held together, because Robert Mann was saying that many people who play this piece come away dissatisfied, feeling it's not a great work. It may be that it's played with too much gravity at the end and too much literal timing. I think that a certain waywardness is indicated by Beethoven in there.

Bob Mann and I are probably going to do a couple of recordings, one of the Delius, I think it is the third Violin Sonata which we played in a concert a few months ago, and the Elgar Violin Sonata. As a matter of fact I would like to do the Triple Concerto sometime, if I can get the nerve to practise hard again. I am getting a lot of invitations from orchestras to play, but I feel I want to creep towards concert performance in my own time and at my own speed. It's very flattering, but I don't plan to kill myself with what would be an unprecedented and unfamiliar schedule of work, even though I've more than a taste of it in the preparation of the Triple Concerto.

I know what you mean by the Americans applauding at each movement in the Aspen recording. This is really because most of the audience, or at least a lot of them, were in show-biz as it were! They weren't used to the tradition of keeping your hands in your lap until the last possible moment.

Yes, I certainly remember playing Tony Lumpkin in *She Stoops to Conquer.* *[This was an excellent school production.]* One of my main impressions too was with my leg up on a table with a tankard of ale, although I can't for the life of me remember leading a chorus at the time! I also remember Robert Williams dying a few years later. *[He was the staff producer who tragically died at a young age.]* Oh my God, and then you remind me of Miss Williams, *[the Headmistress]* saying that I could either be choir accompanist or take the acting part, but not both! I certainly remember the year before I had to go up to Magdalen, which was a great luxury. I think I did absolutely nothing in that time except have fun. I think I probably needed it! It was supposed to be one of those years where I did wise things like read the newspapers and catch up on literature, but the temptations were very great to saunter around and look as if one was working very hard, instead of actually doing anything too much!

You mentioned myself and Susan, with Claudette Colbert in Venice. She came up to me and said that she is such a fan! Again, what a strange quirk of fate and time. Recently Danny Kaye did the same thing. You certainly get the feeling that something is amiss! Talking about ageless wonders, Terry Moore was seen on television recently at the age of 52, looking absolutely great. Some of them do tend to go on for ever. I guess it's bone structure and genes, or something.

I never saw the *London Town* film musical that you mentioned. In fact I missed Sid Fields in the main because my parents were not too hot on having me go to the grubby old Music Halls for a laugh. Maybe I could have the odd snicker in the organ loft at church, but an outright laugh at a Music Hall comedian in the theatre might have been too risqué.

Hope I'll be getting over to England at some point this coming year, since I'm going to be playing probably the oddest role in my life up to this point, an elf in a production of *Santa Claus*. But of course, as befits my present status, it is the <u>main</u> elf in the production! So I shall be across in the UK at some point. I'm not sure when because neither this film nor the one that follows it actually have been pinned down.

Yes I do get thousands of letters and I do have a secretary to help me tackle the fan mail. I used to try and do it all myself, but it is absolutely impossible. You find yourself doing nothing else in the end if you aren't very careful and I get so worried about answering personally that it can go on for ever.

Thank you for your last remarks about *Six Weeks*. The only consolation I have right now is that it is about to come out on cable TV here and maybe people will be able to see it a little more kindly. With a bit of luck, they'll understand what we were up to. Anyway, I must fly, as we all say and I'll hope to talk to you later.

All the best as always from

January 19, 1984

Dear Peter,

Many thanks for your letter which I have just received. I'm amazed to read that the *Daily Mirror* relates my comings and goings so closely, although I do know that they ran some photographs of me from the year 'dot' with my slightly lazy comments attached to them. Regarding your comment about Patrick, *[his son]* he certainly loves to play the piano. Gravitates towards it very naturally, especially when I'm not pushing him! He's a wonderful artist and paints, truly for his age, spectacular stuff. I try to get him to do as much as possible. I would love to fill my house with his paintings and pictures. They are charming and full of that wonderful innocence that we all know about but now have put a lot of it in the basement! He likes to imitate me a great deal from a comedic point of view and, I think, is going through a stage of disappointment that he doesn't get the same effect! If only he knew how many failures I had as a young man, he wouldn't be so daunted! It apparently is a bit of a problem for him. Also the fact that people are constantly coming up to me for autographs. He feels as if he is constantly being looked at and feels in dread of what he says is "being asked for money!"

I saw him in New York over Christmas which was very pleasant. Although spending time with my ex-wife's husband's son's friends (?) was not the most at-home situation that I could have thought of. So I spent many hours moping about lost Christmases with my parents and felt particularly stricken with the vanishing of those years.

I see that you also saw the *Daily Mirror* photo montage diary. I don't quite know what they used in terms of quotations from me. I may have used expletives or not, that doesn't bother me. But I <u>can</u> guarantee that I won't be quoted verbatim, so the expletives wouldn't be-used particularly amusingly which is a shame. I think it <u>is</u> possible to do this! Again, I don't feel the necessity to guard myself when I speak so the inevitable mild shock of what, to me, are 'mild use' of expletives, actually doesn't concern me very much. I'm afraid I have always loved school boy 'smut' and the sheer exuberance of 'playing in the mud', so that is certainly the part of me about which I am in no way reticent or ashamed! However, as I said before, the *Mirror* is not prone to quote me perfectly. The journalist doing the interview was writing things down as opposed to using a tape recorder, which is always a bad sign. Journalists tend to try and gee up what I say with their slightly off-base invention.

I'm amazed that they put in a photograph of my piano teacher. She was certainly my only piano teacher. I had no practical instruction from anybody except her, from the ages of six to sixteen. Unfortunately she instilled very little in me. I thought she was a fairly useless old dear. Her main use was I suppose ... well actually I can't think of one use at all since I didn't get any musicianship from her, merely the ability to read music, which I'm certainly grateful for.

I'm surprised that you felt I seemed happy as a youth. I was, of course, when I was making the effort to ingratiate myself with my peers, but there was an enormous amount of depression. I mainly fought off that gloom by being, or trying to be as popular as possible. But I felt that I had sold out a lot of myself to gain that popularity. After all, I have spent the last nineteen or twenty years trying to get to grips with this rage, fear and grief in myself, through one form of psychiatric application or another! I still don't think I've come to any great conclusions, except to know that it is difficult to shift anything too greatly in myself.

I think you <u>did</u> teach me something, although I am very aware that we were constantly in conflict over matters of harmony and counterpoint and music generally. That situation didn't change at Oxford either and doesn't seem to be any different now. I'm very wilful about the way that I think and feel, so I don't think you should feel that you didn't do anything in those early days. I remember us playing with great pleasure an enormous amount of music together and maybe the fact that we weren't 'too far apart in years' made it difficult for us to be teacher and pupil. I know some of your comments on my exercises didn't go down too well with me, but surely that is inevitable in something as personalised as musical creativity. It's not like chemical equations which are either right or wrong. I'm not telling you anything that you don't know, am I?

I remember Sheila Middleton and Jean Jenkinson. I think Jean had a lot of freckles and a bun, as far as I remember. I remember a lot of other names from that period, people who really got into my gut one way or another, Stella and Shirley -- people I think, from a teacher's point of view, could almost have been viewed as reprobates, but maybe I enjoyed that side of them. Their rebelliousness was something I could really emulate. After all, my main theme was merging colourlessly into the crowd, and yet at the same time, standing out from it. A strangely difficult but enormously urgent ambition of mine at the time!

I'm surprised I didn't answer your question regarding attempting a Chaplin biography, writing script, music, directing and starring in it. My very clear feeling about this is that I would never try and impersonate somebody who has done rather too well as it is! Members of the Chaplin family approached me on doing a film about him as a matter of fact, but the script was so unbelievably sentimental and silly that I didn't want to do it. I don't think I would have wanted to do it anyway and would refuse to play anybody who has previously made a great mark for himself as an entertainer. I don't see the point. I've seen really strange biographies of Abbott & Costello, and, by Rod Steiger, W.C. Fields. I feel that the result was very dissatisfying and totally non-illuminating. I always found Chaplin, when he opened his mouth, to be a strangely pompous man and I've never been a great fan of his, which I may have expressed to you once before. I would not want to play somebody who's lived in the past, or indeed in the present! I've been offered a couple of Mozart films, which I don't think I would want to play. Again, partly because the costume is so ludicrous for me and partly because I don't know that I would really like to do that sort of thing. Mind you, the attraction is greater when people have been dead for a hundred years or more. So I'm not entirely against this, although I can't really see myself going around in wigs and I certainly couldn't wear the costume with impunity! And for cosmetic reasons, my left leg would not be accommodated by silk hose! That would always be a problem, although people who do these scripts never seem to realise that or believe me when I say that it is a problem!

It sounds as if none of my films has been missed in England, except for *Romantic Comedy*. I believe it comes out some time in the future, since I was asked to do some foreign press on it. I have a feeling it will come and go fairly quickly. It is not a blockbuster. *Unfaithfully Yours* opens here in the United States on February 10th. I've just done another one called *Best Defense* which will open in U.S.A. in about six months. I start another, temporarily called *Mickey and Maude*, in April, and the *Santa Claus* film with me, God help me, as an elf (!) about Septemberish in England. God knows what I anticipate playing in ten years' time?! Curiously enough, I was talking about this yesterday afternoon. I give myself maybe another ten years to play the sort of roles I'm playing now, but then when age has set in I'll probably resign myself to character parts or maybe disappear altogether in as undignified manner as I can muster.

I do agree with you. It does seem awful that we are working now with a feeling of imminent destruction. It affects me enormously and gives me a feeling of futility. I have associated myself with a couple of 'ventures' here that are trying to promote the proliferation of views about nuclear disarmament. I don't know what the hell good it will do, but it's the best I can do at the moment!

I think as I said in my last paragraph that I will be over in England sometime in September. I will be there about four months. It could be September, October or November, knowing the film industry. I'll probably be filming at Pinewood and maybe living there or in London central. I don't know at the moment, but either way I'm sure we will bump into each other. Till then, thanks again, Peter, for writing. I will talk to you or write to you rather, very soon.

All the best,

May 28, 1984

Dear Peter,

Got your letter today. I could have sworn I answered your last one in detail but I may have been dreaming! Anyway, lest I start every sentence with "I thought I said", I shall begin anew as if nothing had happened!

I am sort of vaguely considering the idea of producing, directing, starring in, and doing the music for my own films, except that I like to get in and out a little quicker that that. If I find a product *[project]* that is absolutely right for me in my terms and to which I feel I can devote a lot of time, I will go ahead on that idea. Otherwise I think that I will just act in my films and maybe do an occasional score. The one advantage in doing everything including produce, is that one gets to have control over what is going on. The headaches remain the same except that one has the responsibility and satisfaction of making decisions oneself.

No, I was not in the Oscar ceremony this year. I watched it on television like most people. After all, why go unless you are nominated or doing the show!? I agree (with some diffidence I must say, in this town... simply because one hates to speak ill of one's fellow actors publicly), but I do agree with you that Shirley MacLaine's performance, to me, was over the top, although I was highly seduced by the latter part of the film, *[Terms of Endearment]* having been in great aggravation during the major part of it, wondering why people were laughing so hard. Anyway, it's difficult to know or predict what people are going to like... least of all, myself.

I've yet to see *Yentl.* Barbra Streisand is not, as you may imagine, terrifying in real life... although I think she is to some men. In fact, she complains that men find her too powerful. I think she goes for slightly weaker men, so that she can seem more powerful!? On the other hand, I think she also likes to get bullied a bit, which is sort of unfortunate. I don't know if you know that Amy Irving, who was nominated in that film, is in fact in the film I am doing now. *['Micki and Maude'.]* She is delightful... very beautiful and comedically, very adept. Also, coincidentally... Michel Legrand will be doing the score for this film, which I'm rather pleased about. I think he genuinely does some really delicious stuff a lot of the time.

Romantic Comedy may have opened and closed quickly, *[in England]* but it probably did so with no fanfare. *Six Weeks* was in England I know, because my sister saw it, so you have to be quick to catch them sometimes!
England sounds really very dismal. It makes me feel that my visit is going to be more and more gloomy. Anyway, I will hope for the best. It sounds like I'm coming to a rather nasty province of a police state country.

I think you should follow up on that American-made documentary that used some of your music. You really must get on to them about that – although, I guess, as I say that, this is library music and you get a once-and-for-all fee. Right!? I'd forgotten that. It is frustrating, and maybe you are right -- you should get an agent to push things. I don't think you should really concern yourself with things getting too high-powered. Try it!

I agree with you regarding the songs of Andrew Lloyd Webber. I think they are unbelievably dull...although I think a lot of popular music that comes out is really rather terrific. Certainly in terms of orchestration and ideas. I know what you mean about the classic writers, but I think it's maybe a little too early to judge the contemporary ones, but—I know what you mean!

Good to hear about your scars! Hope the rodent will not appear again! *[I had a 'rodent ulcer' cut from my chest!]* See you in England at some point-- in my 'elf' costume! We should have a photograph taken, don't you think? Maybe you should wear an elf costume too!

Write to you soon. All the best,

[We did indeed meet again in the Winter of 1984, when Dudley was in England, making his Christmas film, 'Santa Claus the Movie', playing an elf. "Why ever have you taken on such a role," I asked. "Possibly to give my son Patrick, something he could relate to," was his reply. I am not sure I entirely believed him!

I came to his hotel in London's West End, where he had been complaining about a chesty cough, something to do with the hotel air conditioning after the Californian climate. I brought him a bottle of Owbridge's cough mixture, an old fashioned remedy. He immediately swigged down about half the bottle, several doses at once. I don't know whether it did him any good. But it was such a pleasure to meet again and renew our old acquaintance.]

March 18, 1985

Dear Peter,

Many thanks for your letter which I just received today. I'm getting back to you immediately, since I'm about to go off to New York for a while and things tend to get a little chaotic when I travel.

My sabbatical is progressing quite nicely, although I still don't feel as if I'm not working. Maybe it's because I'm having to go back and forth between New York and Los Angeles. Other factors seem to make it difficult for me to relax entirely, which is slightly frustrating. The upshot of it all is that I'm just thankful that I'm not doing anything... otherwise, I would get harassed, I think. I'm finding it very easy to keep clear of any offers, although if something really wonderful came in, I'm sure I might be tempted. Right now however, it seems very foreign for me to be in front of a camera and I don't know when I will really want to work again. It's hard to tell.

I don't think it's time for my autobiography yet, as you not-too-seriously suggest. I think that will be a while yet, although I should, I suppose, amass material. God knows, not very much of an exciting nature does happen to me, believe it or not!

I <u>do</u> hope that the possible problem with your arm is not serious. It is obviously something that will make you apprehensive until you know the result. *[There was a possibility of lymphatic cancer, but thankfully it was benign.]* I will keep my thoughts with you and hope that all is well. Your two experiences in the operating theatre sound very different as of course they always are, when one is subjected to a <u>local</u> and then a <u>full</u> anaesthetic. I'm sure your arm is very painful... that's the only nasty thing about waking up after that marvellous floating feeling. I remember coming out of the operation on my gallbladder and wondering what on earth had hit me. I hope the problems that this has caused with your music commissions will not be large ones and that you will complete everything in time and comfort. I will keep my fingers crossed. That almost sounds flippant, but you know I don't mean it that way!

Sorry to hear about your disappointment with your latest record album with Chappells. It must be aggravating and disappointing to have them carve up the items in that way. I obviously don't know what is entailed in their judgement of recording quality. They may well be right in terms of similarity to other pieces, because that obviously is a real problem or hazard in the area of parody. *[This was an album in the style of songs from the Thirties and Forties. It was a period with many plagiarism trials and Chappells took out a few numbers, anxious that they might be too close to existing songs.]*

I don't think your letter was pessimistic. It seemed very realistic to me and admirable, so don't berate yourself for that. I think that the music business is an unutterably difficult and frustrating state of affairs and your dealings with it must be very disappointing at times.

Rest assured that I am having an assured rest! I have yet to relax completely, but things are going well. Thank you. There's nothing much to report, since my main object in life right now is to do <u>nothing</u>!

All the best as always from

Letters from Dudley

May 23, 1985

Many thanks for your letter of the 20th of April--the day after my 50th birthday! It's strange how you never think that number is going to hit you, but it does...and of course it has the same wonderfully bleak effect as 30 did all those years ago. Anyway, much to my surprise the day passed off fairly un-traumatically. I had dinner with my friend Susan Anton the night before my birthday and we bled into midnight so that I could be sort of unofficially 50 years old with her. Then I was going to run into a hotel and watch the seconds tick by until I could with bated breath wait until I was 50 -- however I decided to fly to Los Angeles and have a dinner with some friends of mine at the restaurant that I co-own at Market Street in Venice. I had a very pleasant time indeed, which I suppose was 'crowned' by the appearance of 50 girls from the University of California in Los Angeles, in prom dresses, each holding a candle and singing all those awful mundane songs about birthdays and "We love you Dudley" and all that sort of stuff. I blew out fifty candles and took a photograph with them. It was fun -- believe it or not!

Referring to your opening paragraph in your letter, I don't recall our family playing too many games all together, although sitting around a radio at weekends was always great fun, even though the first event was the Billy Cotton band show. I hated that programme with a vengeance because it was always followed by people like Ted Ray or Kenneth Horne or the Goon Show. My mother and I used to play chess, not with a board but with one of those peculiar little plastic carry-around chess sets. We rarely all four seemed to play together but there certainly seemed to be a feeling of some community, especially as we all sat in one small room together most days and nights!

I was so delighted to hear your news regarding the biopsy that they did under your arm. That must have been a great relief for you. It's hard to believe they kept you waiting five weeks for the information. It is amazing what tampering with the arm can do though. Your story about the swelling you get when you play reminds me of the problem that my friend Robert Mann had for a while after he had his gallbladder removed. His arm was affected by the I.V. drip feed that he had connected there, to the point where he experienced some pain and stiffness in the arm for a while.

Glad to hear that *Micki and Maude* received some good reviews. I was sent some of them by friends. I generally don't like to read them too much since even the mildest criticism is like a knife in the back these days. One critic -- Ian Christie, I believe it was, seemed to be obsessed with my size! He had always disliked me and couldn't see what anyone saw in me, --so <u>that </u>I could have done well without! I have to keep reminding friends not to send stuff through the post that is potentially hurtful.

Elgar remains a composer that was so extraordinarily burnt into my heart through early days of Nimrod, minor choral works, and the "Pomp and Circumstance" marches. In later days I've grown to know and love the symphonies, the cello concerto, the violin concerto and although I don't know it that well, the "Dream of Gerontius." Of course I forgot to mention the Introduction and Allegro for Strings which was an enormous favourite of mine. I'm so swept away by this man's music and by a lot of the vaguely nationalistic English composers. It is strange that I've grown into someone who's not at all nationalistic, yet irresistibly seduced by the echoes of nationalism from my youth. I'm not sure that Noel Coward's remark about the evocative power of cheap music was totally right. It's rather like the idea that it's easy to make a funny joke when it's dirty. It isn't actually true. I don't think I'm quite such a Spartan as Glenn Gould, who I don't think appreciated anything other than truly polyphonic music. His remonstrations against Chopin were quite surprising to me.

I read with interest and was affected by your paragraph regarding what you felt mattered in life. I think although music is very important to me, the only real thing that does make any sense to me is a personal relationship or personal relationships, but more specifically the love of another human being in a one-on-one relationship.

I think only with that does the loneliness diffuse itself and the conflict stop gathering. Comparatively I suppose music and work generally are far, far lower down on the list. As I think you know, I have no hopes for an after life. I think in a sense, whatever we are lingers on in some way or another... not in any metaphysical sense but in a way that human influence tends to linger over the years. But it seems to me that we are all the same and all potentially enormously valuable to other people's lives. I have no hope for anything after this life... In fact I think I would rather be appalled by the prospect. I think I like the idea of just vanishing. Then you could really have a good rest!

I have to finish now, as I'm about to pick up my son. He's been playing kickball, which I suppose is our football. He gets very frustrated when he can't get things right the first time, even when it comes to kicking a ball and I suppose he has all that awful competitive stuff to go through for a few more years yet... God help him. Not that I believe in a God or that he would help him! Anyway, if you'll pardon my brazenness...

Good to hear from you -- and terrific news... What a relief! Hope things continue to be OK with you. I send you all the best as usual.

August 6, 1985

Dear Peter,

So glad to hear from you so soon -- and since we are talking about me (!) -- glad you enjoyed *Micki and Maude.* I agree with you on the abrasive quality sometimes that occurs when wilder moments clash with atmospheric and sympathetic moments. But within a farcical film it often seems to be difficult to judge these things as well as one might. I also elect to delegate the directorial task to a third party and therefore give up a certain amount of control in that area. I'm willing to do that so as to not drive myself totally nuts with the director's task as well as the actor's task.

Sorry to hear of the continuing disappointments regarding your music. It seems that so many musicians labor under the discomforts and disappointments of life on the world of business or performance -- I just had a letter from a brilliant clarinettist, Stephen Bennett, who quoted something that Andre Tchaikovsky said to him-- "Like me, you are the chap whom all agree to admire and no one engages."

I was interested to read your postscript regarding going through Dagenham. I must say that I find it almost attractive when I go through it because of the countrified atmosphere. That is probably because I live in a somewhat deprived area such as Los Angeles which has mainly very strange sights to offer. Recently I took Patrick and a friend of mine and her son through my old haunts in Dagenham. I think Patrick was a little young to understand that I had lived there as a boy and the impact it had on me, although he was quite frustrated when I showed him the house where I was bombed out. He was not too clear when I tried to point out a bomb scar on the house. Maybe he knew something I didn't because I realized later when I saw my sister and brother-in-law that I was pointing out the wrong house in the wrong street! I thought that was a nice piece of irony!

I'm still continuing with my sabbatical as well as I can. I seem to be living in other people's places most of the time... hotels and rented houses. Anyway, it's not entirely unpleasant. Hope things are improving with your arm. I'11 write to you soon.

All the best as usual. Sorry if this letter is a bit jerky, but I guess that's the way I feel tonight!

Yours ever,

September 20, 1985

Dear Peter,

Many thanks for your letter of the 3rd of September which I just received. Regarding *Six Weeks...* my sister also wrote and told me that the performance on BBC television had been cancelled. Well, it was disappointing for me too, although as you suggest, perhaps BBC will eventually get round to re-programming it. *[It was announced in the Radio Times, then withdrawn.]*

No, I don't remember too much about the outbreak of World War Two. Of course I was alive at the time, but being four, I don't think it really meant too much to me. My mother, sister and I <u>were</u> evacuated to Norwich, Norfolk during the war. I cannot remember how long this was for... I seem to recall that my father was not with us at the time. I think we might well have been there for about a year or less... it's hard to remember. I do remember making friends with a very nice gardener there called Herbert Harmer, who used to feed me cheese sandwiches at lunch on his wheelbarrow, and infuriate my mother by filling me up with all his comestibles and ruining my regular meals!

I take your point about Essex being very beautiful, especially on its borders with Suffolk-- I did not wish to imply that I was longing for those beautiful sights while submerged in the smog and tackiness of Los Angeles. It is certainly true that L.A. itself is not particularly beautiful, but I've never been drawn to places for their beauty... only for work and eventual familiarity with friends that I've made generally in that part of the world. That is really the only reason, apart from the work, why I live here.

From a scenic point of view it is truly awful in certain spots, but I've never ever been put off by that sort of thing. I'm sure that is puzzling to you, since I know you are very conscious of the beauty of the countryside. I found the beauties of the countryside very minorly consoling in my life and am blind to those seductions, having been mainly concerned with a personal relationship or relationships which seem to have nothing to do with their surroundings. To this point I would add my stay this Summer in East Hampton. The vegetation is lush, the gossip rife. It is truly a beautiful place, but I found myself feeling very isolated, mainly because of emotional reasons, and the beauties of the area were of no consolation at all. California itself is a beautiful state. Los Angeles just happens to be one of those very undecided and mainly ugly cities. There are brief spots of beauty but again, that isn't really what keeps me there. A nucleus of friends that I've acquired seems to be what I now enjoy.

I remember seeing, in recent years, 'The Best Years of Our Lives' and that seeing that the man who has lost his hands *[Harold Russell]* stands out so vividly in my mind. It certainly was a massively urgent and busy score during the beginning of the film. After your comments, I would certainly like to see it again.

[I had commended this wonderful film and its magnificent, evocative music by Hugo Friedhofer. I could never with dry eyes experience its opening --the three ex-servicemen returning to their small town after their war years, and Friedhofer's score for this.]

I agree with you about certain passages in the piano concerto of George Gershwin. The melodic lines are extraordinarily beautiful. I remember hearing them for the first time not too long ago having for some reason avoided the work or perhaps just not knowing of it -- and I was startled by the typical and extraordinary beauty of the melodic writing. In fact, when I played "Rhapsody in Blue" at the Hollywood Bowl, I did about an hour of his music and included the main theme, [from the first movement I believe) of the Piano Concerto. Getting one's hands around that and trying to make it sound like the piano plus the orchestra was sometimes a bit much! And furthermore, I would love to hear the original two-piano version of "An American in Paris." I'm sure it would be great fun. The orchestral version seems to be mildly stodgy, although the night I heard it at the Hollywood Bowl was the first time in many years and maybe the orchestra got a little blanketed because of the atmosphere or just poor acoustics.

No, I never did meet Ira Gershwin although through him I got a doodle that George Gershwin had drawn apparently when he was on the phone to friends or whatever. He used to doodle on pads and left an amazing number of these around the place. Ira

Gershwin during his declining days apparently wanted to let some of these doodles go, and his secretary, who had helped me with the Gershwin research that I needed to do for my concert, let me have one. It was of a black youth standing –it was just a simple portrait but somehow it was thrilling to have something he had done himself -- George Gershwin, that is.

Talking of rare recordings, you mention for instance the one where Frances Gershwin (the younger sister) sings her brother's songs to piano accompaniment. I haven't heard that but am trying to get a friend at BBC to search out a performance of the Grieg piano concerto by Percy Grainger that he made when he was in his seventies or eighties -- about the last recording he ever made. It was so full of mistakes that the record company, after about nineteen prints of the performance, stopped issuing any more. However, I was lucky enough to hear it on BBC Radio one day. Also, the comment that Benjamin Britten had made about this performance, saying it was the most romantic performance of any work that he had ever heard! I must say I agree it seemed to be a passionate display... perhaps not so much a display, but a passionate 'expression' of a man who knew perhaps that today was his last. The number of mistakes is truly dazzling and even a computer would find it hard to keep up, but the spirit was extraordinary. If I ever get a tape of this, I will try and get you a copy, since with all its mistakes it is a massively moving performance. *[He was never able to do so.]*

Well, I guess I've come to the end of my facts and figures for tonight so I will bid you adieu again. All the best as usual from the 'strange smog' of Los Angeles,

November 8, 1985

Dear Peter,

Briefly... thank you so much for your letter. I'm going to be in London, hopefully at Claridge's from about November 23rd, for a couple of days. I'm there very briefly since I'm just in for the Santa Claus premiere, which is on the 24th. Then I'm on to Spain and France to do some publicity. Please give me a ring at Claridge's if you can and I will certainly do so if I can get to your house while I'm there. Sorry about the grammar of this last sentence, but I'm running a little, trying to get things ready before I go.

I just had to answer a few things in your letter. Yes, I do get nervous tension before playing music publicly or doing anything publicly. I generally try not to calm myself with the very real fact that the people that are listening are just people. That sort of thought doesn't make too much of an impression on me!

The terrible truth about the Percy Grainger Grieg performance is that I don't know if I've been sent the right one <u>yet</u>. I listened to the concertos briefly when I first got them but neither of the performances seems to be the right one. It's really very frustrating... what I really need to do is find the person that brought up the Benjamin Britten quote and find the actual programme on which it was done.

The Santa Claus film comes out this Xmas, but don't expect too much. It's one of the blander performances I've ever given. Mainly because the elf psychology seems to lead one in that direction! However, I think it is an entertaining film for children...although I don't think it is a classic as I must have said millions of times. It may well be able to do a little time on the public front, hopefully for everyone concerned.

I'm going to run now. As I say, I'm in the middle of getting ready to go to London. Hope I'll be able to say hello when I get there.

Hope things are well with you. All the best as usual,

[In my latest letter, I had given my honest opinion of Dudley's two current films. I felt that 'Santa Claus' was rather too bland while 'Best Defense' was quite chaotic, and that elements of the one could be transformed into the other, to the advantage of both! This is Dudley's reply to my 'review'.]

February 20, 1986

Dear Peter,

I think you are quite right that a bit of cross-fertilization between *Santa Claus* and *Best Defense* would have possibly done both pictures a bit of good! However, I must say in defense of *Best Defense* (!) that the script read really wonderfully when I first saw it. Unfortunately the director in his insecurity, forced us all, I think, to push performances too hard with the surprising result that even Eddie Murphy was over the top.

As I read the increasing excitement of your review, I must interpolate that it is very hard to predict the outcome of a film from the time you read the script to the time you see the finished product. I was very disappointed with the result of *Best Defense* when I saw it. In fact I said to a companion (who was in the film) after the first two minutes (during a screening) which I thought were excellent, "From now on it's all downhill!" Unfortunately, my words were only too true, even though I'd said them very jokingly.

One of the problems of the film was the constant crossing backwards and forwards into different time zones, as they might say over here. But more than that, the relationship between myself and my wife in the film was almost completely omitted, much to the film's discredit.

I quite agree with your views on *Santa Claus...* that it was much too bland. After every take I used to scream with the frustration of having to play a character that was almost devoid of anything except good nature. Mind you, I didn't really see the opportunity to do a great deal more. I had no hopes of inserting any great comic inventions, feeling that the character was going to be mainly a fairly one-sided affair. This might have been a miscalculation on my part, but it was hard to do otherwise somehow.

I did the film for the money and Patrick...in that order! I felt the film script was sufficiently good to interest me. I knew it probably didn't have too much chance to be a classic, but went on in any case. I was mildly intrigued by the thought of doing the special effects stuff, although the actual work in the film studio when doing those things is particularly humdrum.

Anyway, the upshot of all this is that I've taken my year or more off and hope that I will be more stubborn on a set when I do another film. It seems to be that most comedians get more controlling as the years go by... probably in response to a relentless clock! I may well turn into a prima donna on the set instead of my usual compliant self.

Yes, I'm afraid my sabbatical has been rather dour and not productive. Not that sabbaticals are supposed to be productive, but I felt that I would delight in producing music of some sort. Therefore, I am creeping back very cautiously into film work. I have three to four film projects that seem to be mildly up for grabs and I'm sure I will be settling into something this Spring. One thing is certain... that I'm going to be even more wary and pig-headed about anything I do now. I can't afford to do things for money (!) and I can't afford to do things that I don't throw myself into entirely again, even at the risk of exhaustion. The trouble is, or rather the consoling thing is, that it's even more exhausting not to involve yourself, as you can imagine.

My plans for coming to England do not seem to be very clear. My sister wants to see the King's College Cambridge Festival of Carols at Xmas, which is about the only time I may be coming, --although as I write this, I realise that I am tentatively scheduled to visit London for a programme with Bernard Levin, which will hopefully reunite the four original members of "Beyond the Fringe" 27 years after it's first performance! There's a depressing thought for you (!)... the length of time, not the reunion! So -- maybe we will be able to say hello this next time. I hope so. Sorry I didn't make it this last visit, but truly it was truly a brief in and out moment.

Please don't feel that you went too far in your film comments ...they are very justified and very much a part of my own thoughts.

All the best from

April 17, 1986

Dear Peter,

Many thanks for your letter of the 22nd of March. As I approach my 51st birthday with some awe and amazement, I can safely say that I don't quite know how I got there! But here I am, still alive and kicking. *[Dudley was involved with Brogan Lane, whom he married in 1988.]* Brogan's son fractured his wrist today and we went to the surgery department of the emergency room at the hospital to talk to the receptionist about our obligation to stay or not. She announced for some unknown reason that she was sixty but felt as if she was twenty one and by some peculiar quirk of fate her body had strangely fallen apart! She was a very merry soul... somehow I feel that I know what she is talking about now, although things are not falling apart yet, but... we will see!

Regarding *Best Defense*, yes... Eddie Murphy's part did read very well in the original script and is bound to the main body of the story by the fact that he is driving the tank in which the mechanical part that I redeem is placed. So, at the end of the film there should be suspense as to whether the part will work and protect the tank from the invading helicopter -- which of course, as in all good American movies, it does! Unfortunately, I don't think any of us could foresee the problems of going back and forth to each story. Even more unfortunate, I think, is the overkill that was plastered onto the playing of those roles. However, that's the cinema for you. This and other experiences make me feel that I should be more of a prima donna in my films. I might get a reputation that will sag over the coming years as I interfere more and more, perhaps to the point of directing my own stuff, -- although, I don't feel that I have any talent for, or desire to, do it. I'm amazed that *Best Defense* has played so long in London. That is truly amazing. It might be the lure of Eddie Murphy...who knows? He's had some success recently with *Beverly Hills Cop.*

Patrick enjoyed 'Santa Claus' very much and I think was secretly flattered that I gave his name to my character.

Addressing another point you made in your letter, curiously enough I seem still to be 'bankable.' I think people are imagining that somewhere there lurks in me the success of *Arthur* or *10.* They may be right... I'm certainly hoping that something will come up that will fire me with the same enthusiasm. It's about time for this dog to have his day again, I think! These things I'm sure are cyclical and I have no doubt that it will be possible to be, as they call it, 'hot' in this town again!

It's interesting you said something about *Amadeus.* In some ways I would have loved to have played the part. Unfortunately, my identification with the part in 'Arthur' may have mitigated against them using me... although I noticed that Mozart in the film seemed to have three-quarters of my laugh at his disposal, which seemed rather bizarre. I was hoping that I might get a call from Milos Forman regarding this, but never did. I remember Robin Williams, who is a great stand-up comic here, mentioning the fact that the film was being made and saying how good I would be for it. I agreed in many ways and hoped for an approach at least -- one that I could perhaps decline. However, nothing emerged.

One of the real problems was of course the costumes, -- because, with my gammy leg, there is no really satisfactory way of disguising the peculiarity of my left leg, as the foot moves inwards from the vertical. Even if you wear a false piece on your leg, the angle of the knee to the foot cannot be circumvented. Also, they might have felt that the possibility would be that the audience would feel that I was playing the role for laughs.

It would certainly have been a wonderful role, but then again... I have no real regrets -- in the same way that I honestly don't think I should play Hamlet. Although it would be a wonderful role to play, as any comedian would tell you (!) --I know what I can do and can't do... although even that is not entirely true, but that's another story! I do agree with the actor's method of conducting in that film. Amadeus was sort of silly and I felt that a lot of musical things were jokey and played down to the lowest common denominator of musical appreciation in the audience.

I understand your fears for the future. They do tend to grow almost imperceptibly as time waltzes on. Perhaps it's time to shake a fist at the heavens and plunge on. But then your many frustrations in the music composition are enough to break anyone's spirit. I hope you will not feel thwarted overly by the constant procrastinations you seem to run up against. *[I was going through a bad time but it didn't entirely last!]*

Your remark about being wet-eyed during the final chorus of Brahms's Requiem certainly rings a bell with me. Certain music does not fail to have that same slow, expansive effect on me, where my heart swells and the tears inevitably come. Certain sequences have such a comfort for me that they are hard to bear. It is like the ultimate embrace that one really deserved much earlier in life! As you can see, I don't mind getting purple now and again... I don't care any more.

Your post-office girl remarking on my last letter --"Is this the real Dudley Moore?"-- there is another Dudley Moore apparently, or was, in Hampstead where I used to live—of course. An architect who, when I finally phoned him up because he was getting mildly cross for the obvious reasons, said "I keep getting phone calls here and letters, because people think I'm you." Maybe he is me... and maybe I'm an architect! Perhaps that is the root of my angst!

All the best as always,

September 22, 1986

Dear Peter,

You could have knocked me down with a feather or at least something not too much heavier than that when you mentioned your idea for a film for me... namely regarding an older person taking on the spirit of a younger person. I haven't seen the old film you refer to-- *Vice Versa*, but I must take a look at it. Anyway, the point is that I have recently agreed to do a film with Tri-Star Productions out here, concerning a man and his son who inadvertently exchange spirits by some device or other. So... there's a turn-up for you! If I can't play Peter Pan, I will at least it seems try to do something on the same lines.

I must interpolate at this juncture, that I have just received your letter of the 3rd of September, or the 3rd instant as my mother used to write in even her most informal letters. Sorry that I might have given you the idea that the previous letter had gone astray. I'm surprised actually that I hadn't answered sooner, but events in the last months have kept me rather busy, to the extent that I am going to drop practically all extra-curricular activities-- meaning charities of one sort or another. I've also been writing out the *Beyond the Fringe* music for the publication of a book by Methuen London Ltd. It has not been great fun having to write out some of this stuff again, even though I suppose it's not that horrendous a task. I have just objected to having to set down on paper things that were fairly free in their style and interpretation when I was on stage. That and the appearance of a book called *Musical Bumps* purportedly by me has kept me busy. The latter is in aid of the National Playing Fields Association charity and contains some very amusing anecdotes about music and musicians and some introductory remarks by me for each chapter.

All these things were occurring, plus a fairly disastrous cruise on the QEII-- mainly because of the harassment of people on the ship demanding autographs and photos almost continually. Also, a concert in Honolulu for an organisation here called "People for the American Way," (which tries to keep the fundamentalist religious zealots at bay) --then I found the sponsor of the event a strangely invisible man, to the point that Brogan and I escaped to a neighbouring island for what we thought would be a small respite, only to find that we were in the middle of a heat wave, spending several nights in uncomfortable humidity. We finally turned tail and came back to L.A. I'm also involved in the publication of a book called *Voices of Survival in the Nuclear Age*, incorporating the views of lots of individuals whose professional life or aspirations are in many ways very different. I'm in good company...the Pope, the Dalai Lama, Indira Ghandi, etc. (!)

Anyway, the upshot of all this is that I have been fairly lax in responding to mail and thus I apologize for not getting back to you sooner on the subject matter of your last very interesting letter which was sent in June.

I was as usual intrigued to hear of your musical activity and of course those memories very associated with various pieces of music. It all runs so deep.

Yes, I do have a secretary to sort out my mail. But there is no problem with your mail getting through, since my mail gets to me regularly --through his good offices -- again as my mother would quaintly put it!

<u>Certainly</u> I would love to meet all the other *Fringe* members, although...nothing has been reported to me since the first invitation from Bernard Levin some time ago. I would certainly make the journey at the drop of a hat,... however, I don't think everyone shares my alacrity in that area. I'm sure that Alan Bennett is probably being the most reticent, even though he, I would imagine, is the one member of the ancient quartet who resides pretty consistently in London. I'm not sure what we would have to say to each other at this stage. Alan I know, is not too keen on what we did in the show, saying that we've all done better things since. That may or may not be true, but I still think it would be fun just to see us all together. I would certainly love to have it as a souvenir. Maybe the pathos of the four Musketeers at fifty is too much for some of the members to take... I don't know.

It is nice to know that our views about music's power and potential are very much the same. It's good to know that you are able to keep writing, although I can certainly sympathize with your desire to have something dramatic to get your tooth into. I almost wrote, in fact I <u>did</u> write 'tooth'... I meant 'teeth'. This is no disparagement on the tooth or teeth situation, but it's certainly amazing how they or it figure or figures in the process of time!

I heard a remark the other day which may have been on something as controversial as MTV (Music Video), which is a cable station here --the quote was that Beethoven had said that there "are no bad tunes... just bad orchestrations." He may be right, having had such a high perception on other musical dilemmas.

Talking of Woody Allen as you did in your last letter, I was much moved to see again his film *Manhattan*, which I must say moved me immensely. Even more than the first time I saw it. I have a feeling when I first saw it I was not quite in the mood, although I did enjoy it. He is an extraordinary performer and writer. I think in a curious way he is as great <u>in his own style</u> as one of the people he truly admires -- Marlon Brando. Unfortunately with *Hannah and her Sisters*, Brogan and I and her son sat front row at the side of a cinema in New York. We were just able to squeeze ourselves in. Everyone at that angle looked as if they had pears for behinds and it was hard to take any of the drama or indeed any of the comedy seriously. Maybe I'll wait until I can get a video version of it. I must say that I didn't like Michael Caine's performance too much. I found it very mannered, but then I always do find his performances that way except for his very first film, *Alfie*, which I think embodied him and a character almost perfectly.

I have not much to report in terms of myself except a mild malaise which I think comes from a length of inactivity. The prospect of doing a film does not exactly thrill me I must say, but I will pursue the notion because I feel the alternative is somehow worse. I cannot necessarily assume that my life will be fulfilled by film work. It is certainly an economically viable way of life, but it is sometimes hard to find the perfect thing to do. As I end this letter, the sight of a vampire on TV, about to plunge his fangs into a young woman's neck, has been replaced by disco dancers. Television is certainly more than enough to keep my mind alive these days!

We seem to end our letters very similarly, but I'm sure we are both sincere. It would be nice to say hello and meet again. I'm sure we will do it sometime.

Meanwhile all the best,

November 11, 1986

Dear Peter,

Many thanks for your letter—once again. I'm writing this because I often find that as I read your letter I tend to want to respond to things straight away and obviously catch the first crisp breath of spontaneity! Interesting what you say about *Vice Versa*, since there is a version of that initial story which is, as I think I mentioned before, extant at another studio. I've read the script, unannounced, dare I say, to the studio-- and found it rather a good story. It certainly involved a ruby or, I seem to remember, some sort of skeleton head with magic properties, so there the similarities are certainly more apparent to the original. With the one that I'm supposed to be doing, the notion is much the same. The device to change spirits is slightly different and the story is more a love story rather than a love story plus mystery and chase, which is involved in the *Vice Versa* script.

Frankly, it's hard to know how to choose between these scripts, especially when they are both on the same subject... and when neither one stands out infinitely more than the other. However, the plan is to pool a lot of ideas with a lot of writers and see what comes out. Normally I would be very much not in favour of so many cooks stirring this particular broth, but the specific ideas that are needed for this story are so universal, that it will be good to have the input of a lot of people. I'm sure we all have things we would have liked to know at an early age.

I'm, as I said before, being mildly apprehensive about doing this film, since I haven't been in front of a camera for so long. However, I have a feeling that the energy surrounding this idea will carry me along... at least I hope so.

I have been getting much satisfaction from musical things. It's somewhat pathetic of course that because of my elevated position in the celebrity world, that people of all sorts and conditions will be pleased to in some way collaborate with me. For example, I recently participated in the celebration of the 80th birthday of the Director of the California Chamber Symphony Orchestra, Henry Tamienka, who has been in his time a pretty well known virtuoso violinist. I don't know much of his work or playing, so it's hard for me to judge. He did play briefly at the celebration, but it wasn't really enough to judge him by. The only thing seemed to be that he had a very large vibrato, which sometimes a string player seems to get when he grows older. Anyway, I found myself playing the first movement of the Spring Sonata by Beethoven with Isaac Stern! It was a very interesting and worthwhile experience. Luckily for him, I think, and certainly for myself, I have been playing with much more sensitivity and ear, if you like, in recent years,...so that I think that my approach in recent years is more intelligent than in the past. I think that is due to a development of, --dare I say it, sensitivity.

I also played with Angel Romero, a very well known classical guitarist. I say well known, but I don't know him myself that much, not being a great classical guitar follower. But he seems to have played with everyone but was delighted to play with me since I had done *Arthur* and other films that had amused him greatly!

Luckily again, my musical expressiveness has I think, certainly in my own view, gone up in recent years -- so we hit it off very well playing, incidentally, some songs by Manuel de Falla, which he had arranged for guitar. He was delighted and so was I by the performance. In a way it seems mildly pathetic that because of my celebrity I'm given these golden opportunities, but I certainly am grateful and bask in the warmth of the communion with these people. I met Janos Starker, the cellist also, who knew of my work and had seen a television programme I had done at the Hollywood Bowl, playing Gershwin's "Rhapsody in Blue." He was very flattering but cautioned whether I would be taken seriously as a musician, even though he felt that my performance of the "Rhapsody" was probably the best he had heard! I'm not sure that I would share that opinion which may have come out in the flush of the evening's diplomacy. However, in a sense it doesn't matter whether I'm taken seriously or not. I get the chances and it's fun!

Related to this is the publicity I'm giving to a book called *Voices of Survival in the Nuclear Age,* compiled and edited by a man called Dennis Paulson. I seem to be the only one of these 120 people that can get on TV and talk about it. There are a number of Nobel Prize winners and extraordinarily important and interesting people who have contributed to the volume, but they don't have a chance in hell it seems to appear before a camera. I do because my face is known. Mind you,... in the process of doing this stuff I'm getting pretty knowledgeable on strategic defense initiative and all allied subjects. I think my rebirth has commenced!

I wish I had the energy and motivation to write and direct my own film and compose the music for it. Right now the subject does not present itself. It may do with the passing years... it seems silly not to use those facets of my productivity, but as yet nothing has presented itself. I would say however that I am grateful for a flowering of consciousness, which makes my eyes grow a little bigger and my mind stretch and yawn and think a little more than it's been prone to in the past.

I was a little dismayed to hear the continuing frustrations regarding your musical compositions. It must be such a deadly grind getting people to perform what has taken your blood and sweat to produce. It seems the course has never been too smooth. Regarding which, I'm not surprised that the BBC didn't respond to your letter regarding *Six Weeks*. *[I had written to protest that after the sudden cancellation they had never re-programmed it.]* I now and again get a comment from a fellow actor who sees the film on cable, which heartens me to a great degree.

Well, regarding the waterfront home-- the move is actually going to be made soon willy nilly. We are going to get in there and probably live on the top floor for a bit, while the rest of the house is being seen to. I am tired of paying out fantastic rentals for houses or hotels and if it means being in a sleeping bag for a while, it doesn't really matter. We are going to attack the fort and make a stake! I'm looking forward to getting back, although the house is very different and the area is almost new to me now, since it's been over two years since I left. The inside is looking terrific and I'm sort of excited at the prospect of using the recording studio in there. I hope to God I don't let it lie fallow. I hope that it will really inspire me...we'll see.

Thanks again for your letter and let me echo the sentiments that you expressed in your first paragraph. Don't feel that you have to write back immediately, because I've written back immediately! I just wanted to get you my feelings hot off the press. Not that they are necessarily that hot!

Meanwhile all the best as usual from

PS. Leslie Halliwell's article and comment raises the whole notion of censorship. I don't believe we can protect ourselves or others from criminal activities by censoring our art. I think it would be possible to say that one might be influenced by *King Kong* to jump off a top of a building as easily as to go out in the dark with a chainsaw after seeing *The Texas Chainsaw Massacre*. The link is tenuous...there will always be people who are influenced by the most horrible of scenes, but there will also be people who might well feel like stabbing someone after seeing a film about monastery life!

Left: Dudley's first composition, "Anxiety." (c.1947)

Right: Dudley as a choirboy. (c.1946)

Left: Class 1B, Dagenham County School. Dudley is second from the right in the front row.

Below: Dudley as Tony Lumpkin, on the table, in a school production of "She Stoops to Conquer" (1953)

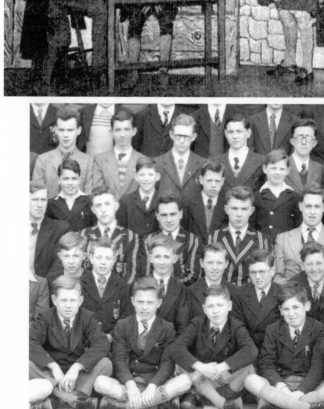

Above: Dudley at age 18.

Right: Dudley as Deputy Head Boy in striped prefect's blazer. He is in the center.

Above: With Marie José at Southend-on-Sea. (1953)

Left: Playing the piano. (1953)

Right: Peter Cork working on a musical score. (1958)

Below: Dudley and Peter Cork in Edinburgh. (1958)

Left: Sharing a laugh with his Parents.

*Right: I*n the back of his Maserati on Baron Road in Dagenham.

Left: On the beach outside his Marina Del Rey home in California

Letters from Dudley

[I had said in my previous letter that we tended to present an idealised picture of ourselves when writing. This is Dudley's response in the first paragraph of this long letter!]

January 13, 1987

Dear Peter,

Interesting point you make about presenting an idealized account of oneself and all attendant problems on paper, not measuring up to fact when an actual encounter ensues. That I'm sure is certainly the case. There's no doubt that one tries to turn an elegant phrase, even if it's dictated!... and wants to present oneself in the best possible light. Even when the worst light is presented, it is done with a degree of poetry that one hopes is a mitigating factor. Maybe I should drop a caveat that I am certainly not the person either of us think I am...either individually or together. However, a lot of it is true and I suppose changes from moment to moment, ...which is why we all feel that we present a false picture. I don't know that we can really expect ourselves to be totally consistent. That might be a convenient way of making everything we feel and think not come up to scratch.

Regarding the Stern and Romero performances-- yes, I think they were recorded in an amateur way...perhaps on video tape. I'm mildly embarrassed by some of the juvenile slips I made, but then aren't we all, all of the time.

I haven't as yet received this recording, but may have access to it when I visit the man to whom all this concertising was dedicated. I will be interested to hear it, although I know that apprehension will gnaw fairly unpleasantly at my stomach. Not that I have to prove anything I suppose, but I know where the glitches occur.

It made me laugh -- the prospect of my letters being left to someone. I don't really mind to whom they are left _if_ they are. They are a collection of thoughts that certainly are a little inelegant and ungrammatical at times, because I'm being a tiny bit spontaneous and not the greatest proof-reader of all times. But I was flattered and pleased to know that you feel a greater sensitivity in my letters. I certainly feel it in my life so it is natural and good that it is to some extent reflected in these communications.

I'm mildly flustered... the word 'vapours' springs to mind-- when you talk of my ferocious *[musical]* technique. God, I wish it <u>was</u> ferocious like that of Horowitz or others of his ilk. I have a facility which I never quite push to its limits... perhaps afraid of the inevitable wall I will meet. A wall that is only dissolvable with immense application and stamina of spirit and enthusiasm.

Letters from Dudley

[We had spoken of the classic black and white films such as 'It's a Wonderful Life' being coloured.]

I must say that I don't get too worked up about the colorisation of these old movies. I quite <u>enjoy</u> it to a certain extent. Perhaps there are shades of subtlety in the black and white photography that I miss... but I'm not sure that it is a 'purity of expression' that is a little overprotected. I'm sure, however, if I made a film in black and white, that I would feel a little nervous about it being interfered with. I must say that the computerized versions of these things don't seem that extraordinarily awful... and I'm sure they won't in years to come. Maybe it's as harmless as the stereoification of old mono recordings. I think that the ear is now so used to the lushness and appropriateness of stereo recordings, that one doesn't object to that process being applied to old stuff... even if it is a false dimension if you like.

Funny you saying that I <u>must</u> have an angel over my shoulder. I used to play angels continuously when I was a lad at school...perhaps being influenced by the tapping on my shoulder! Well, I can't really condone that thought, although God knows it's attractive. About as attractive as the thought -- and I mean very attractive -- that my mother put into me... namely that I must be a reincarnation of Byron (!), because I have a club foot like he did and was born on the day he died 111 years ago. ONE ONE ONE being of course some magical formula in her mind! I also at one point nurtured the idea of being a genius when I was very young. It made me feel rather special, I suppose to counteract the feeling of insecurity that was at the root of my self. There was a certain magical quality about the word which gave me that polarized specialness, that people who can't get on with their own lives often adopt. Over the years, I've realized that it is a term that is not particularly meaningful. It can often be a quirk of genes... an ability for infinitesimal application and desire for work. I remember when I mentioned this whole area to my friend Robert Mann, the violinist, that he felt that the word genius was often misused. He applied it to Glenn Gould, who he felt was a genius, because he could memorize photographically and play very musically a whole piece that he had only very recently encountered. In the end I suppose it doesn't matter at all. As Schnabel felt, music should be practiced in an atmosphere of love and with patience. I think that is all that is required of us. The titles we extrapolate for that sort of diligence can be applied later if ever.

My sister it seems was equally aggravated by the disappearance of the *Not Only...But Also* segment on the BBC reminiscence programmes. However, there is a very unsinister explanation. Peter Cook and I asked for that programme to be withdrawn, (since we weren't very pleased with it) and at the last moment the BBC had to do it. They had assumed that it would be alright with us and were going ahead with the transmission, but then were told by our agent that this was not the case, since we hadn't been consulted. Even if we had been, we would not have wanted it to be shown, since it was a programme which we felt in no way showed our paces to the most favourable degree. There were other segments and extracts which we had been asking to be shown, but one section of the BBC it seems just does not have access to the other. So, that's the situation there.

Cary Grant's death was very unexpected, although he was in his eighties and normally one would not be surprised. But he looked so damned healthy. I was glad to have known him slightly and received his friendship. His raucously dirty jokes were always fun and a part of him. His wife Barbara is a great beauty and a very sweet woman. I feel very sorry for her, although she seems to have taken his death stoically... probably realizing that it would come at some point. His appearance always belied his age, which is why I think the shock was greater than in most cases. One funny story occurs to me. I have been afflicted with a case of vitilligo in recent years, which means a crowding of pigment in certain areas of my face and a virtual disappearance of it from others. The areas where the pigment has disappeared are very pink and almost baby-like in appearance. The other areas look dark, giving me sometimes the appearance of a washed-out raccoon! Once when I went to a party where Cary and his wife were present, he looked at me and said, "Have you had something done to your skin to make you look so young?" I didn't really want to tell him that it was something that was not overly desirable at that point that had contributed to this mildly youthful appearance. Perhaps the lighting in the room didn't make me look so tired as it normally makes me look.

The other anecdote of some dubious distinction was that I had bought a pair of very beautiful earrings for Brogan, which had cost me a small fortune. They were delightful and both Brogan and I were very happy with them. I can't say that earrings are my first choice of a present for anyone, but it seems to be that these pieces of jewelry have a traditionally profound—traditionally -- effect on the heart of a loved one! Anyway, we were going to some horseraces at Hollywood Park with Cary Grant, his wife and various other people. The earrings on the way got lost and Cary and Barbara shared in our horror and disbelief at this mild tragedy. So his death perhaps symbolises regained earrings... I don't know! Anyway, I'm sure he would find that funny.

[The following paragraphs continue the discussion of censorship in the previous letter.] Perhaps the lovemaking scene has become a cliché... beautiful bodies writhing on the bed. They are becoming rather a bore to those people who have no great relish in the whole affair. I'm not sure about the argument that says the more restrained love scenes are more effective. It may be more fashionable in an atmosphere of repression to applaud such moments in the same way as historic qualities of old American heroes and heroines are more applauded... since they were never explicit. The openness of expression of people is sometimes intolerable to the major part of the world, hence the reception given to a film such as *Six Weeks*.

Well, yes I do think there is a difference between the killings of *Friday 13th* or *Texas Massacre*. There is something different from those moments when Christians were thrown to the lions or gladiators battled to the death. That was <u>real</u> death... I think people do know the difference. If ever you see a documentary where people are actually shot, it is much more nauseating and disquieting than the situation in a film where things are presented like a fireworks show. The other night we were watching *Life goes to the Movies* and there was an appalling section where American soldiers or sailors were applauding the demise of an enemy bomber. It crashed into the sea just beyond them and they were obviously excited. One can understand the excitement and relief, but to see it in front of one's eyes made one feel quite nauseated.

The Iran and Contras affair is obviously going to be quite a long and drawn-out bore. It is hard to believe that the President of the U.S.A. knew so little. How can one believe the pseudo-sincerity of this salesman. His mealy-mouthed dripping reassurances offer me no solace. Talk about the Emperor's New Clothes! Lots of people are pointing out this same issue, so it's not a silent issue respectively withdrawn... (so I suppose the Emperor's New Clothes comment is not appropriate.) *[This was a reference to Ronald Reagan]* The ridiculous convolution and diplomatic slaloms make me pine for a gentle sword to cut through. Everyone has so much to lose and so much is being protected. When nations make their secret deals, they are doomed to policies of concealment and deceit.

Xmas is over here, although we had a lovely party at the nearly finished house here at the Marina. Patrick was in Italy skiing like some jet-setting sleaze-bag! We are here among wood-shavings and plaster, but it is fun and we are experiencing great joy in these rapidly more beautiful surroundings.

I will hope to write again soon. Meanwhile have a wonderful New Year. It's amazing to think you are sixty now, however that's my next big one... so we don't seem that far apart.

All the best as always,

P.S. Couldn't help mentioning that I just saw *A Run for your Money* -- you may have mentioned it to me in one of your letters, I don't know... but it was a charming Ealing Studios comedy with Donald Houston, Alec Guinness and Moira Lister, apart from other very delicious characters that seemed to run through the script. The tone of the film was helped greatly by the inevitable charm that only a male Welsh choir can exude. The sound of those voices enjoying music for its own sake and especially at the end of the film when accompanied by an as yet unblitzed Hugh Griffiths playing the harp, was true pleasure.

I suppose the film had all those ingredients, primitive and sophisticated, to grip me at the core of my heart. The sound of exuberant and loving singing. The sight of those old trains with their sturdy compartment doors and the almost palpable smell of the engine stack. The sweet enthusiasms of those naive yet wise Welsh miners in the film, struggling gamely amidst the exotic trials of London... retaining somehow their zest for life and innocence-- and honesty. The sight of houses near the platform of the station at their home-- those houses that I would have envied when I was a boy. How lucky they are to live near these ingenious and awe-inspiring locomotives, with their screaming speed and reliable bodies, hurtling through stations at breakneck speeds. Well, I can tell you, it took me back almost to the point of seeming to recognize the coats they wore. These raincoats that made me think of my father's raincoat. He gave me his overcoat, which I wore with great pride for many years, until somehow it vanished-- like his watch... which at a value of three dollars got out of my safe keeping. That I regret almost more than anything regarding things that I have. I used to love that watch...it was so thick -- unchicly thick, with the inscription on the back running something on the lines "Given to J. Moore after 45 years of service." Well, those rewards would have seemed like the jewels in the Tower of London in those days.

I felt both elated and amused and revivified by this film. It took me back so far and so hard that it was difficult not to feel an assortment of emotions. Mainly a distinct feeling that my roots had somehow vanished. I found myself at the very end of the film, with the sight of the railway platform and the house overlooking the rails, saying to myself "I have no roots." Of course I do and I was remembering them only too clearly...yet realizing in a strange way I am uprooted and living in a foreign land, which only appears foreign when I see a film like that. It reminds me of days of wonder, excitement and mystery. It's not that everything has become pale by comparison, although there is an element of that process in what I'm saying. However, I remember Peter Ustinov saying on a programme once that he had no particularly fantasies or <u>extraordinary</u> pleasures in life...merely because he felt that – whether he said it or not - they were things that were available to him. He did not have to be in that condition of endless longing, although that still exists in me and my musical self. Maybe that's why I don't work as hard as I should on my music... otherwise the feeling of longing might be satisfied! Anyway, far from being blasé or jaded, I think my priorities have changed somewhat...and probably when I think about it, for the better. Those days in London seemed to be the temple of excitement and fulfilment and were extraordinarily exciting. Now to work on my music and other things can be equally fulfilling, if not quite as exotic. I suppose that I feel that since my heart is so strongly drawn by this film, that somehow that's what I should go back to ... but it isn't. I cannot return to those days...but merely savour them with the melancholia, nostalgia and pain that were bound up in those days. It's not as if things have become too easy. Somehow they have become more demanding and it's more important for me to fulfill myself in ways that I hadn't really dreamed of when I was younger. Maybe I'll look back on these present days with an equal nostalgia in years to come.

It's curious that in some way I have constructed an environment here that can enclose me... not exactly in an English embrace, but with aspects that can remind me of those things that I either had, or longed for, when I was a child. One of my favourite places to sit in my house is in the living room opposite the fire, where I can see an old primitive painting that I bought twenty years ago in London, and look at and listen to an old grandfather clock (from 1760) that I purchased recently. It's a sweet pine creature, a wonderful reliable patriarchal figure, rather like those locomotives, but with less passion! I sit watching the picture, the flames and the clock ... listening to that calm ticking on a beach in California... as I watch the old Xmas tree that I put up with ornaments. A Christmas that we never had when I was at home in Dagenham. We just had paper chains that went diagonally across the ceiling. Those were our decorations and nothing else! It is wonderful to be in that atmosphere and to listen to carols of church choirs as sung by choir and orchestra of Caius College/Cambridge. It is odd to have all these things about me in one strange place yet it has become my home. I can imagine the English Downs outside the window if I will, or that locomotive steaming through Chadwell Heath station. I suppose nostalgia has me by the throat... I'm going to loosen it with an excursion out of this mood. I'm grateful for it, and I don't know if I could live entirely with it. It reduces me to a stagnancy that merely reaches out unsuccessfully to the future. I used to feel that that longing was a positive force. In many ways it is, but I know that it is a romantic temptation to feel that one can only long for things and that those feelings alone are significant.

I'm going to end this strangely romantic tone poem! I wanted to write as soon as I saw the film however, since it was so sweet, heartbreaking, funny. I'll talk to you soon.

[The last sentence in Dudley's deeply felt postscript was to come true in a way that even he could not have imagined! In the January of 1987, I received a telephone call from Thames Television. They were mounting 'This is Your Life' for Dudley in Los Angeles. Would I consider flying out there to take part in it? I had recently received the previous eight page letter which Dudley's secretary had transcribed. When he was approached by Thames, my name had come up. It was not the first time that Dudley had been a subject for the show and this one was to run across two weeks, the only time it ever did so. They would make use of Hollywood celebrities and wanted some 'ordinary folk' to leaven the mixture.

I was initially very doubtful about accepting. I was sixty and in the process of leaving my London flat and severing the last educational link. My Mother was then in her late eighties, not in a good state of health and needed my care in the Folkestone home. However she pressured me to take this 'chance of a lifetime', and so I arrived at L.A. airport, to surmount the chaos of entering the United States and to be met by a stretch limo, almost as long as a street!

Dudley's sister Barbara had also arrived from England and a day later we were at the ABC television studio, eight hours before the show, little sleep beforehand, suffering heavily from jet-lag. We were to be kept at the studio until zero hour and I wondered how I could possibly cope, for the time would be in the middle of the night according to my body clock. However I was suitably impressed to see all the stars, Bob Hope, who had been born in England, looking just like he did in all those Road films, songwriters Henry Mancini and Sammy Cahn, Jackie Collins whom I would sit next to after saying my piece, Cleo Laine, John Dankworth and Chevy Chase who would do a glorious jazz improvisation with Dudley, and Robin Williams who raised up a storm in the greenroom, entertaining the guests.

Waiting for my entrance behind the curtain was terrifying, especially as Robin Williams went minutes over his allotted time. But eventually I was introduced by a recorded phrase about Dudley's sight-reading ability and I stepped through the curtain, to be greeted by an astonished smile and a bear hug from the great man himself. Luckily the footlights obscured the huge audience and adrenalin took over. We had all been given a script, based on our telephone conversations back in England. We had to attempt to keep to this, prompted by Eamonn Andrews in what was to be one of his last shows. It was not easy for a non professional but I understand I acquitted myself well. The show ended with Bob Hope making the star kneel, and dubbing him 'Sir Dudley of Dagenham!'

Afterwards there was a celebration and I could see how happily Dudley fitted in to this environment. There was a freedom and friendliness which seemed to relax everybody, as contrasted to the more stressful British approach. Dudley was obviously loved by a vast host of people. I had the opportunity of a couple of days in L.A. after the show and delighted in seeing the film-star homes in Beverly Hills, the Chinese Theatre where all the great movies were premiered and the stars put their hand-prints, (I was keen to find Deanna Durbin's print as I had great affection for her work.) The Universal Studio tour was only a stone's throw away from the Holiday Inn where I was staying, King Kong, Norman Bates' Motel and all.

But best of all, I could spend a day with Dudley. Early in the morning, two days after the show, Dudley drove over to my hotel and a halcyon day was to follow. His home was in Marina del Rey, with views of a fine Pacific beach. It was a traditional house which seemed to be bathed in white, the furniture all stripped pine. I was particularly impressed with a fine banqueting table, a crevice running down its middle where flowers and house plants were actually growing. Don't ask me why, but it had something of the atmosphere of a cathedral, with sudden eyries, openings in the white walls, where you could look down at distant levels, Dudley's pianos were there of course, where he would begin every morning playing Bach, and an actual recording studio. It was with great pride that he showed me the master bedroom and a wardrobe that covered two sides of the walls, the sliding doors opening with a swish to reveal an Aladdin's treasure trove of clothes. Dudley was married to Brogan Lane at the time and I had met her at the show, very impressed at the way she master-minded the contestants. She was away on this day but I met her later in London. I liked her immensely and she obviously cared a great deal for Dudley. The next Christmas she found the whereabouts of Dudley's Dagenham piano and had it shipped over to the States, a nostalgic surprise for her husband. I was so sorry when this marriage, like the others, came to an end. "Dudley's music means more to him than anything else in the world," she confided to me when he was out of the room and I think this was true.

That evening we went to the restaurant which Dudley co-owned with his film-producer friend, Tony Bill. It was an enchanting place where he would often play jazz standards to the happy customers. It was also the place where 'This is Your Life' began. Bo Derek, his glamorous co-star from '10', had appeared and presented Dudley with the famous red book. Well, maybe he wasn't that surprised!

He insisted on driving me back across town to my hotel. "I can't risk you getting lost in an L.A. taxi," he said. It was sad to say goodbye and return to my own country, but I had been so happy to see him in all the splendour of his new and adopted home and his brilliant career and style of life.]

[There now follows the first letter after my wonderful visit to Los Angeles. I had written to Dudley about the great warmth and friendship I sensed in his life there and the 'sunny ugliness' of the L.A. scene.]

March 18, 1987

Dear Peter,

Yes, there is warmth and sensitivity here. A sort of openness that you don't get in England. That was what first drew me to the States. 'Sunny-ugliness'... I like that phrase very much. It's certainly not inapplicable to this odd conglomeration of architecture, people and freeways. But it is the friendship that I cherish... The ease of people that are willing to confront without being undiplomatic or just plain nice.

It was good to see you too, even though you were obviously in some state of fatigue and bewilderment... having been dropped rather ungraciously into this strange but inviting lap. I need the comparative gentleness of these people here -- it seems to feed me. I think I have become more gentle over the years or at least have allowed myself to show it a little more.

I've just been startled by a strange gnawing noise in my office --my cat Sadie was behind me, trying to eat an envelope! Patrick, my son, arrived about an hour ago. He's not exactly at ease and has requested some time on his own, possibly to get to know where he is once again. His discomfort is very difficult to deal with, but I think he will thaw out in coming days.

I've begun filming this week. It's aggravating to try and watch my diet as usual. The film is not in perfect shape yet, but over a period of three weeks we have invested a lot of time and energy and enthusiasm. I hope it will stand us in good stead during the shoot. So, I suppose this letter will not be too long. I'm talking to you as I read your letter, which is what I like to do. That way the reactions I have are spontaneous and fresh. I'm in the office area of the house, looking at some new furniture that has gone down in the sunroom area of the house. I love all these terms that the decorators come up with...sunroom, den, patio, deck. I am not sure they are entirely right. I think I like words like study and library better. But...

I think your point about losing roots is well taken. I might well have felt this just the same if I had remained in England. It is sad to read in your letter of the mutilation of England's green and pleasant land. It's hard to believe that it's happening at this distance, but probably unrealistic not to think so.

Your remarks regarding my letter are fascinating and insightful. I have not had many opinions expressed about my mother, except perhaps by someone whose name is almost identical to yours... Peter Cook, but whose character is certainly different. As I get older, certainly those gentler characteristics from my father's character are entering me, or at least displaying themselves more often. Talking of which, I think I have reached a point in my life where all the uncertainty and upheaval I feel is because I have to rediscover what I really want to do yet again! That could be anything from playing the piano to reacquainting myself with early or Victorian literature. God, I don't know! No doubt the answer will scream slowly and gradually over a period of time until it can no longer go unnoticed.

This letter threatens to be really a mild hiccough in our correspondence. I have a few things that I am worried about doing and thus, am tending to dip from one subject to another. Hope you will forgive me.

God, how amazing with Joan Greenwood dying at the age of 66. It seemed only yesterday that she and I were doing a scene in that fairly strange film that Peter Cook and I did called 'The Hound of the Baskervilles.' I found her irresistible and she always seemed to have the same character that satisfied me personally and completely. I was never bored with hearing that mildly superior, ever so faintly disdainful tone, disguised with that succulent sibilance. *[I too remember the making of that film. It was the only time I ever met Peter Cook, when he and Dudley were cutting it in an editing studio off Wardour Street]*

That's about all my news for the moment. I'm mildly obsessed with getting this film done, which means that my poetic imagination is severely curtailed presently! It was so nice to see you. I'm glad we were able to talk, at least a little.

I will seriously consider coming across to England for what you suggest-- a two to three month sabbatical sounds a good idea.

I hope you will find some relaxation after your traumatic move from your London address.   That is going to be hard to adjust to.

[I had sadly left my London flat of seventeen years, to return to Folkestone and look after my Mother, then in her late eighties.]

I wish you as always the best,

Letters from Dudley

May 27, 1987

Dear Peter,

I will be replying to your letter as I read it, since my thoughts tend to fly off very quickly...flower and die very quickly also!

I too wanted to attend the 50th Anniversary of the school, *[Dagenham County High]* but for one reason or another --I have a feeling due to filming -- I was unable to come. Certainly your description of Dagenham's mythological drabness was interesting to me, since I too have found I rather underestimated the beautiful greenery that hits one when one enters the area -- certainly of Parsloes Avenue. You may certainly be right that it is the contrast with the rest of London that perhaps makes Dagenham look rather more desirable. I don't think I noticed the greenery in those days. I was more interested in the eyes of young girls, or in the eyes of London in the shape of twinkling lights in inviting rooms of restaurants and clubs.

Yes, I found the school much smaller when I looked at it from the outside on one of my many tours. Has the clock not elected to work again...the one in the middle of the building? It seems to have stopped for years, which seems to be a great shame.

God, how disappointing when you tell me that there were only about 200 old students at the occasion. It sounds like the rather dismal feeling I got when I went to a reunion a few years ago. Certainly my own particular year of 1946 was very poorly represented. We had one meagre table of stalwarts. Those faces that I wanted to see were just not there anymore. They're all out there hiding somewhere no doubt. God, I'm startled by the notion that I might have attended the event by way of a helicopter...that is such a wonderful notion! Also as you say, it is nothing that I could have possibly anticipated being in the wind in my days of 1950. *[There had been a comment in the London evening papers that Dudley would arrive by helicopter.]*

Yes, I remember Alan Coggins and Bettie Owen. *[two former students]* I remember her voice and certainly Alan's *[piano]* playing, which at the time of my school days seemed very calm and enviably mellifluous. How funny that you were inundated with sermons that day. It sounds like an old Speech Day celebration that is corrupted into-- if you'll pardon the expression—'an evening of worship.' All eight verses of 'For All The Saints'!... This sounds almost like the time when the cello section of the school played 'Frere Jacques'. Oh my God, plus a recording of a Handel duet (!) *[before my days!]*...this reminds me of pre-prayer morning, where your selection was considerably brighter I seem to remember and we had the good fortune to hear very lively and uplifting work.

Your walking around the old buildings of the school seems rather like some Gothic invasion of the graveyard. Perhaps in these circumstances we don't live old times so much as regret the passing of those days. Yet, we are also reminded of the mild horror of those days. I'm clouded with a multitude of reactions to all of this.

Miss Fletcher is still around?... I don't know why I'm surprised at that. She seemed, although very lively when I knew her, as a teacher, somewhat older that the rest of the people. I'm glad to hear that she is still in the land of the living. Hal Cooke I certainly remember... I seem to remember endless charts showing the different sorts of clay in different regions of England. Hardly anything to keep a young boy alive.

You almost bowled me over with the report that Sydney Russell, *[the director of the Kingsley Hall Community Centre]* was at the reunion. I don't know why I'm surprised...(he must be getting on now!). Your description of him sounds as if he hasn't changed a bit. I always felt that there was a passion that he had sat on with Methodist murk. Whenever I complained to him of my illiteracy, he, I must say, encouraged me with the words, "Think of the delights you have to come," rather than a rebuke that I "should have known that all along" as it were!

I'm not surprised to read that you were shattered after all of that. It can only be a dazzlingly dismal retrospective --we have all gone different ways. Perhaps it is a desire to hang on to some bonded past that makes us go through the pain of an attempted companionship.

I know what you feel about the beauty of England when it comes so astonishingly upon the eye. I'm sure the rebirth of the year with its extraordinary beauty is enough to pull nostalgia from any heart. The longing for peace and beauty (as well as maybe mortality) is both heavy and light in our goals at these times. My only problem with the English countryside is perhaps this very thing. I've always felt daunted by the almost inexorable repetition of beauty that nature is able to assume. However, we shouldn't worry... a 'Nuke Nature' plan is under way!

I loved your description of *Song of Love [a film about the life of Robert Schumann.]*. It sounds like those inevitably bad films made about composers. There are so few good ones around. I think *Amadeus* suffered from a not very informed musical approach. The only time I've seen some subtlety is in *Autumn Sonata* by Bergman, where a Chopin Prelude is played by mother and daughter in contrasting ways. I truly cringe when I hear things like, as you quote, "Now the crescendo Clara," or "now the rallentando!"

No, the Barry Norman interview didn't take place at the house, it was held at a residence where we were shooting the *['Like Father, Like Son']* film in Studio City. I have now finished filming on this new film. I feel exhausted from the convolutions of this film and the script. I think we have done well, although you can't really tell. It's been so much work and effort and yet now we are now in the hands of some other rather more wayward spirit. Perhaps we can tie it down with more sensible editing and a continued passion. We'll see!

We have a new member of the family... a Keeshond dog. It looks rather like a little grey raccoon right now but grows into something that resembles a small chow. It's a lovely little dog that we call Chelsea. I don't know quite how we came to that but we did. Its deposits seem endless wastelands of crap and pee, which we try to contain in voluminous pages of the *Los Angeles Times.* It has already conquered our hearts but no doubt in twenty years time we will look back at this little creature and wonder whatever happened and why it was so pretty and is no longer with us.

God, I'm beginning to sound morbid. I don't feel it, I must say, but there's no doubt that one starts to think of these things along the way somewhere.

I think I told you of my immediate schedule. I have two concerts at the Hollywood Bowl July 10 and 11. I then have in August a concert with Itzhak Perlman and Yo-Yo Ma with the New Jersey Symphony Orchestra doing the Beethoven Triple Concerto again. Then in the Spring I do the *Mikado* in Los Angeles. A film I wanted to do with Brogan has fallen through unfortunately. They were willing to try and raise money for myself and her to do the film over a period of two months, but then wanted me obligated to the project if they were not able to finance things with her attached. I feel that's rather a neat way of stalling for two months and then getting someone else who has something of a name. I, therefore, with no regrets abandoned the project, even though I felt the script was one of the best I've seen in years. I felt that Brogan was so right for the role, especially since her problems have been so akin to the girl in the script... whose mild retardation causes endless and mildly exotic problems. Brogan's galloping dyslexia certainly causes a great deal of difficult moments, but her heart is gold and that is all we seek. Besides, the thought of another film project right now certainly appals me.

I seem about to have an argument with the Inland Revenue Service in England. They want to make me domiciled in the U.K. because of my talks of missing England in the newspapers! Unfortunately, I'm going to have to fight this since I feel very much domiciled here...although I, certainly, as we have discussed before, feel the need to see more of England than I have in the past because of the 'lack of completion' in that area.

I'm going to stop this rambling letter right now and have a mild snooze before I go off to do some work on the film. As I said, I feel mildly apprehensive about what the result will be.

I guess the thing I want more than anything right now is for my house to be completed and everyone out of it, so I can sit down, do some work and not have people banging and tapping everywhere. It's driving me mildly nuts!

So, till the next time, thanks for your terrific letter as always.

Affectionately,

Dudley

P.S. Feel like chucking in the towel re the L.A. Philharmonic concert but will persevere. The house is like an ant farm right now with workmen & such. Trouble is, can I let up — and work in this unfinished environment? Answer, NO. I need bookshelves and storage, a floor in the 'den' (!) and a fireplace in the living room. I suppose I want to suffer!

Letters from Dudley

December 4, 1987

Dear Peter,

Sorry to be so long in getting back to you... I've been inundated with paperwork and also pre-production madness with my new film which is a sequel to *Arthur*. Yes, I did get the two letters that you sent before the present one. I'm sorry not to have been specifically responsive to them. Maybe mail has crossed in the post. I think I must have mentioned that I played some of my film music at the Hollywood Bowl plus narrating "Tubby the Tuba" and also playing the first movement of the Beethoven Triple Concerto. A potpourri, as you can see (!) -- followed by jazz for about three quarters of an hour.

Yes, I do remember the *[Violin]* Elegy that you wrote for me at DCHS *[Dagenham County High School]*. I'm not sure that I really played it to anyone's satisfaction, least of all my own. But I remember the Walton Violin Concerto was enormously influential on all of us at the time.

Thanks for your congratulations regarding *Like Father, Like Son*. It seems to be hanging on very well, although it certainly is no *Ghostbusters*! Presently, I'm in New York as I mentioned before filming a sequel to *Arthur*. *[Arthur on the Rocks]* I think it will be fun. The script is a wonderful development from the original and in many ways gives me almost more opportunity than the original, which is hard to believe. Anyway, we will see...

I've counted my chickens before they hatched so many times that it doesn't really matter if I make any prognosis anymore, it seems!

The Los Angeles earthquakes have not touched us too much at all recently, since we only experienced what must have been comparatively minor tremors. My house has been almost reconstructed from scratch. It is resting on a box-like structure which theoretically makes it 'wobble' instead of tear itself apart in the event of the inevitable 'big one'!

My sister told me about the awful disaster you experienced with the hurricane recently. It seems that the disaster certainly took its toll on England in general. It is strange to think of all the losses that were incurred, namely trees. It certainly must have been the last thing in the world to anticipate. It's hard to believe one thousand trees down in Hyde Park!

I think I almost agree with you on the Mrs. Thatcher re-election situation. A glimpse of her on television is enough to turn anyone's stomach. She is so extraordinarily priggish and self-satisfied it's rather chilling.
I know what you feel about life proceeding on without events. With your present situation, your mother being so restricted and you of course meanwhile, it must be difficult to feel that you are actually doing something. *[This was the start of the four year period of caring for my elderly mother.]* Glad however to hear that some of the recordings are coming through despite a messy mix.

Glad you enjoyed *Lovesick*. *[This earlier one of Dudley's films had just turned up on television.]* I'm fond of it, although I'm sure it doesn't go at the hectic pace required for a successful comedy nowadays. I think I explained before that I felt the lack of threat from the characters at the end in the psychoanalytic society was the thing that probably diminished the believability of the whole thing.

Interesting what you say about Michael Tilson Thomas and the Gershwin "Rhapsody in Blue." I was rather mortified by his pianistic knowledge of it before I knew he had actually played it in concert. He was showing me how to do certain things and being strangely wayward, yet almost too dry with it too. He is a showman in many ways... I haven't heard enough of him to judge him, but I would think that in the "Rhapsody," it is hard to know exactly what the tempi are. It's such a patchwork piece, even though it has wonderful melodies. I would like to play it again with more confidence and elan. I agree that the music should really reflect Gershwin's intentions, but I have a feeling that this is one piece where they weren't too extraordinarily fixed. He probably thought about it quite a lot, despite the recording we have of him doing it.

Things are fine with me here, although difficult. I'll perhaps explain later, when I have more energy at my disposal.

Brogan has given me a series of wonderful old records. She wanted to find out who my favourite pianists were. So I now have recordings of Rachmaninoff and Josef Hofman. I'm looking forward to hearing them. I just read a book by Josef Hofman that was very instructive and interesting regarding piano playing. His attitude seems to be that of any other great teacher or player that I've ever heard of... relaxation and a sort of ad-hoc technique, where one had to be aware of the hand's naturalness and comfort while playing. My ambitions in this area do not seem to be huge. That's probably just as well, since I tend to dally and not attack things too much. Maybe that will change, but I can't leave it too long!

I'd better stop now, since I have so much to get through. I send you my best regards as always from a rapidly chilling New York. We'll be here until Xmas, when we'll go to Brogan's family in Virginia...then on to Colorado skiing with the kids. I won't be skiing myself... a broken leg would be a disaster right now! However, a few quiet days alone reading and playing will be nice.

All the best,

March 21, 1988

Dear Peter,

Just got your letter of the 18th of February. No--I try not to read articles about myself too much, because I am still not used to criticism. Obviously, people seem to be obsessed with the fact that I come from Dagenham, that I am five foot two inches in height and the unlikeliness or otherwise perhaps of my position out here in California. It sounds from your description, like a rehash of an article that came out in Woman's Own magazine years ago. It certainly does seem a little on the late side!

I was sorry to hear of the closure of the last cinema in Folkestone. It seems strange that it now does not possess a cinema. The decay and anger that was described in the article that you sent me seems in no small way to embrace such sad assassinations of old buildings and times. The article incidentally was rather startling. It does seem as if England is trying to emulate the problems of 1984. Your, quotation, "Change and decay in all around I see," seems ominously pertinent.

Yes, your final notes are sombre and pessimistic, but I welcome them. I think English people are comforted in some strange ludicrous and eccentric way by the dark beauty of the prospect of death. The only prospect I don't relish is that of a declining body with pistons seizing up and carburettors shortening! Anyway, let's hope at that time an even more splendiferous technicolor ecstasy of life will prevail. No doubt it will. Something to assuage the Godless pain.

It's almost as if Great Britain is trying to become a little empire again in a way that is so much more sinister and mediocre than we could have ever hoped.

All the best,

May 2, 1988

Dear Peter,

Many thanks for your letter and congratulations. I'm happy that I'm happy!

I agree with you, the clips that the Thames Television put together were not too appetizing. In fact, they were thought to be rather dim by quite a few people. It was a very boring and safe selection, I'm afraid. I am particularly touched by your reactions to the Jen Etherington article. I'm afraid that the other things to write about do not come into the area of general interest in these impoverished assessments. Thank you for your support--that sounds like the end of a political campaign, but is meant sincerely as gratitude for your seeing a little more than surface dust.

[The film, 'Six Weeks', at long last arrived on our television screens.] I'm delighted by your reaction to 'Six Weeks' and your appreciation of the music, which certainly took it out of me when I wrote it. I loved the film for all of its tendency to excess and felt that it was a compelling and very thoughtful and feeling tale that was meant to show that people could enjoy themselves as much as possible until whatever end they were faced with. Interesting that you talk about opening the credits with the theme rather than silence and speech. As a matter of fact, it was a concern to the producers that there was at least 45 minutes of film before any scored music appeared. There was source music of course, played as background music for the party, but scored music was actually not used until well into the film. Yes, I did do the orchestrations, using conventional instruments apart from a synthesizer which I used as a sort of electric piano in the background.

In answer to your question at the end of your letter... yes, I do enjoy your letters enormously and don't have that same feeling of incipient exhaustion that comes sometimes with the advent of a circular -- which happens now and again to me. I'm always interested to hear your reactions to things, even if it means near despair at the efforts of our charmer, Mrs. Thatcher!

Arthur on the Rocks comes out probably the second week of July and looks very good. Let's put it this way... I didn't feel like chopping myself when I saw it, so that is at least a good sign! I think it is good fun and quite moving at times... which is all I can ask for. Gielgud is terrific in the situation and I think the film is a delightfully substantial development of the characters and humour.

The Mikado has been and gone. I did ten performances which were really quite exhausting, although I enjoyed doing it and would not have missed it for the world! Especially the opportunity to learn such a greatly written song as "Tit Willow." In fact the whole end of the operetta is delightful, with Koko wooing Katisha in a most disgraceful manner! There is talk of doing it again in a couple of years' time on Broadway or in London. All of these prospects are pleasant, but not really practical. I don't feel like doing it is the basic problem!

I bid you goodbye as I sink in this rapidly expanding mass of paper that I find myself in. It's a truly day-to-day chore, although unfortunately I don't attack it on a day-to-day basis.

Hope we'll exchange letters soon. Meanwhile, thanks again and all the best,

Letters from Dudley

August 24, 1988

Dear Peter,

I generally answer your letters as I go along, since I can normally deal with each point with more energy. But your last letter made me pause for thought, as you were describing your reactions to my interview with Esther Rant Zen. I'm not sure either what point I was making! Peter Cook phoned me and felt that Esther was determined to make it seem that I had given a lot to the world despite unhappiness in my personal life. He was truly amused by the way she wanted to gee me up and make me feel that my complaints were not too real. This I suppose is the wonderful English way of brushing things under the carpet and the reason why I found analysis or therapy here in America more attractive. However, I have not restricted my life or bound it up with self-searching alone. Although again,... I must confess with great ease, that a lot of my self-searching has been very central to my life and helpful in clearing the way to the atmosphere where I can work and look for that ideal relationship in music that I obviously yearn for. You mention this in your last page.

I'm not sure what my feelings were when I did the interview except I was struck by her determination to remind me of the good things that I had done. Of that, I am very grateful to her. My complaints about my childhood will probably always go on, but I do accept responsibility for myself now and I don't blame my parents for what happened. I quite see their dilemma and pain, their horrendously troubled and anxious lives. So I have no problem in accepting where I am. I do know quite specifically that I want to do certain things musically more than anything... and perhaps, in acting combined with music. I'm hoping to do this in a film called *The Piano Player* by Anthony Burgess. Moments of happiness have been many for me. Mortality does have a sobering effect, and the thought of one's body gradually falling to bits is rather ghastly to ponder.

Your letter was truly interesting, and your reactions to the programme were truly fascinating... but rest assured that I am not indulging in some sad concentration on the past. It's something that comes up endlessly in interviews and perhaps some day I will actually vomit over the person interviewing to give them a clue that it may not be the best subject matter for me to embark upon yet again!

The film *Vice Versa* came out before *Like Father, Like Son*. Sort of an arrangement whereby we had the U.S.A. release first and they had the rest of the world! Due to the similarity of the subject matter, some deal had to be struck it seems, so that we all thought we were having the better part of it!

I'm not sure whether I'll be over for the opening of *Arthur on the Rocks* at Xmas. I am rather disappointed at its reception here and am convinced more than ever that I really do know nothing about anything, when it comes to the commercial prospects of a film. Lots of people who have seen it liked it, but the critical response has been fairly miserable on the whole. I don't care actually and it makes me feel quite entrenched in my proposition that sixty percent of the entertainment critics are recovering alcoholics! This sounds like sour grapes and it probably is, but then again, I don't mind a sour grape every now and again.

I'm looking presently at an acrylic-bound piece that I wrote when I was about twelve called "Anxiety." I'm sure you know of this 'magnificent' work! It is funny that it has been bound in this way so comparatively luxuriously. On the other side there is a piece which reflects my passion for the sequence, which was obviously my first erotic inroad into music. Somehow the inevitability of the sequence is what we hope for in sexual encounters!

I'm presently transcribing a couple of records that I absolutely adore: "Concert by the Sea" by Errol Garner, and "The Oscar Peterson Trio at the Shakespearian Festival." This is something I should have done maybe forty years ago... trying to get a bit of their muse under my hand. Well, the truth is that I didn't, but now I have the desire. It may be a little late in the day... but I'm keeping my fingers crossed that arthritis will not stop me flying the way they do in their improvisations.

I'm very content right now with an obvious qualification which comes from life continuing on inexorably and demanding more attention. Although I don't know what that means quite yet!

I hope I'll see you soon. I think it would be nice to come across to England at some point and say hello some of my friends and my sister. It seems a long time since I've been.

I'm going to stop now since I am going to do a little more piano work. Thanks again for writing.

All the best as always,

Dudley.

P.S. Sorry this is a gauche letter in some way. I would smooth some of the seams if I wrote by hand - which I do rarely now, it seems.

D,

Letters from Dudley

[One of Dudley's greatest talents, indeed at the heart of his being, was his ability as a composer. He worked mainly at the keyboard as might be expected from a jazz musician, and there is a touch of Rachmaninoff, but his compositions have great melodic charm, often with considerable poignancy and depth underlying them.

This is most noticeable in the fine score that he wrote for his film, 'Six Weeks'. It is the one serious film that he made, about a little girl with leukaemia, and he poured a heartfelt passion into it. But it was savaged by the critics which hurt him tremendously and he never returned to this style. It was barely shown in England and I caught up with it much later on television. I had heard the beautiful melody which runs through it, which is in the cassette Dudley sent me when recording the score. The thematic motif is probably the best thing that Dudley ever wrote and I understand it was played at his funeral. It certainly always brings tears to my eyes. In my previous letter I inquired if it would be possible to re-cut the film. It ought to start with this fine melody at full orchestral strength and plunge straight into the story instead of a lot of extraneous material. But Dudley said in the following letter that with copyright and such it would just be too expensive a project. So sadly this film, and what could have flowed from it, is one of those 'might have beens'. But this poignant melody will always remain to enchant us.]

January 26, 1989

Dear Peter,

Sorry to have been so long in answering you. I can only suggest that it is all of the goings on with Christmas and the New Year that have led to this unaccustomed silence.

There isn't much to report here. I'm still hoping to do the film *Sketchlife* with Brogan, although time marches on. I seem to have been waiting for a period of two years for this darn thing to coalesce.

I am putting together an LP of some ballads, and I hope to have a very nice man called Kenny G guest on them. He is a very good player and is willing to be a part of this venture, although of course I don't think he realizes that when you've done a hit record as he has, sometimes it's not possible for a manager to release his artist in the literal way he contemplates! So much for my activities projected (and non-existent!).

I so appreciate your promptings regarding *Six Weeks*. It would be nice to do a new edition of the film, but unfortunately producers have the last say in the cut of a picture. They will generally put pressure on a director and others involved to do it their way, because they feel they can sell it better...no matter how erroneously this situation arises. For me to get hold of *Six Weeks* and redo it would be a major job and I would have to finance it myself. If we started at the point where I meet the little girl, we would lose something like 45 minutes. I don't know if it would actually be that much, but I do remember that the first musical cue doesn't come in for 45 minutes, so perhaps I'm muddling it up with that. I take your point about cutting the beginning down a little and in fact it was always a worry that things seemed to start off slowly. It would be nice to think that people would be ready for something richly romantic, but I'm not sure this is true. Certainly from the results of my films in the past, I have no way of knowing what works and what doesn't work anymore!

Arthur on the Rocks, I believe, comes out sometime in February over there... That seems to be the threatened date.

I too, was very disappointed with the *Roger Rabbit* film and walked out after about 45 minutes! I didn't find the thing too fascinating, too funny, too charming or whatever. Certainly not enough to keep me in the theatre. Perhaps it is the lack of humanity in the film that is essentially depressing. I know that the technical aspect of it certainly blew people away here, which is not anything to be too surprised at.

I'm glad you caught up with *Like Father, Like Son.* Of course the ironic fact over here is that we had the first showing and had to sacrifice that position in the rest of the world. The fact is also, that *Like Father, Like Son* preceded the other production. It's hard to know whether our idea was original or not. These things seem to come in clusters and get made in a hurry...everyone wanting to do a film about one theme or another. *Big [the Tom Hanks film]* was very charming, but really to be fair, on another theme-- although the idea of a young boy in a man's body was certainly a comparison that should be made. Anyway, it's hard to know what went awry or if anything did!

No, I am not playing *Dr. Who.* In fact I hadn't heard anything about it. The papers that printed that had been badly advised. *[The press had criticized him for attempting it!]*

Anyway, I'm glad to hear that the *Santa* epic and *10* are prime television transmissions on BBC and ITV during Christmas. I'm not sure that I would want too many people to see *Santa Claus,* but I'm glad it still exists in a way...certainly for young children who like their diets bland. *10* Has always been a favourite of mine and will continue to be so. I think it does stand up in its comic parts very well.

Your trip to the Yorkshire Dales sounds as if it was wonderful and the description of an idyllic time very beautiful. Peace at the Marina peninsula has almost the same charm, as long as one doesn't look outside!

You mentioned that you saw *Like Father, Like Son* towards the end of your letter.. Yes, no doubt the aim was towards the youth market in the States... although I would have thought that some appeal would have been possible in the area of people who, like myself, wish to remain 16 or somewhere around that age! I'm not sure that being in films is the most intellectual pursuit, but it seems to suit me until such time as I become somberly inward looking.

Interesting, that you remarked that one of the critics said I should stop being 'loveable' and start taking on a really nasty character. I don't know what it is, but I'm not really attracted to really nasty characters. This may be what's stopping me from playing Richard III! I guess I'm just a humane individual! I really don't see much fun in portraying that sort of character. They should perhaps --the critics, that is-- realize that I'm already a fairly unsavoury character and I'm trying to redeem myself in my film roles!

I'm going to end now, much as I began, which is literally just pacing the boards here in the house as I read and re-read your letter. Meanwhile, I send you all the best,

[signature]

P.S. Sorry this seems merely to be a catechism of replies - I will generate more interest perhaps in a later letter, although things seem to be down to a crawl here. It is not unpleasant - but it is perhaps a tad unnerving to allow time to tick away in its quiet, unrelenting way.

Letters from Dudley

November 20, 1989

Dear Peter,

Just got your letter—for which many thanks. By the way, although Brogan and I got to the Lake District, we never did get to Keswick. I must say that the drive was the most spectacular that we saw or achieved... whatever the right word might be. It was the most beautiful countryside and we were on our knees with gratitude seeing wonderfully translucent sheets of rain and the countryside that seemed to be carved out of a storybook.

We passed through a village and I'm damned if I can remember the name of it. It was absolutely wonderful, however, and we spent a few minutes looking around there. We took a lot of photographs while we were in the Lake District, but of course they in no way whatsoever gave any indication of what we had seen. The results of our photographic efforts were rather flat compared to the rather extraordinary vibrant effects when we only relied on our eyes. No doubt I'll be back at some point to see England again. It seems to be a different place altogether once one gets out of London.

I'm glad you enjoyed the Connaught dining room--it was rather frightening how those waiters seemed to dominate the whole event. However, I wouldn't mind going back to that hotel again. In some curious way it reminds me of a quaintness and diplomacy that I really rather relish at my age!

Letters from Dudley

[I met Dudley in London and he took me out to dinner at this smart restaurant just off Piccadilly. It was very hot and, overcome by the warmth, I took off my jacket. Immediately an unpleasantly supercilious waiter came across and told me to put it on again. I was breaking the house etiquette rules! It did not matter that I was dining with a Hollywood superstar. But as always it was so good to catch up with Dudley after all those letters.]

Thank you again - and I mean really - for your remarks on my music. I'm so grateful that you enjoy what I've done. I've been trying to get a sort of master tape for the waltz number that I think you mentioned in the letter and I've been doing the damned thing for days it seems. It always seems to be going slightly wrong here or there, or I am finding something dissatisfactory. Anyway, I'm going to persist.

Yes, the earthquake in San Francisco was pretty awful and we are getting some fairly alarming warnings here in L.A. I live on the beach, which I'm told is going to be an area prone to 'liquefaction,' where sea and sand combine in one vanilla splodge and one's house maybe quietly gurgles under. I have torches, or flashlights (as they call them over here) everywhere...including gallons of water and provisions which are meant to sustain after the 'big one'! I didn't actually feel the tremor of the earthquake in San Francisco, but Brogan was at the Toluca Lake house and felt something happen. She was outside and saw the pool water suddenly developing waves. Anyway, we hold our breath a little bit right now until we all forget about it... which probably is going to be soon if we have any luck. The terrible thing is that it could happen in thirty seconds or thirty years.

Glad you enjoyed *Dead Poets Society*. Robin Williams can really be quite extraordinarily funny, but sometimes to a point which can, to a newcomer, be almost savage. He also has a soft side, which I find irresistible, I must say.

I will look out for the Deanna Durbin film *Spring Parade*. I'm amazed that you haven't seen it. I certainly remember "Waltzing in the Clouds," since my sister Barbara had quite a passion for that song, and I remember the other two songs you mention as well. I'll see what can be done about getting a copy of it over here.

Certainly, I would love to look after your manuscripts if ever you kick a bucket or two! However, maybe you would have someone in the family who would do so for you. But if it's a question of this stuff going up in smoke as well as you, then I'll be happy to hang on to it. In fact, I would be very flattered.

Vladimir Horowitz, talking of 'kicking buckets,' kicked the big piano bucket in the sky, to mix my metaphors. It seems strange to see a TV special on him -- this strange adenoidal figure, who had one of the most unattractive manners. A strange creature who brought forth extraordinary sounds from the black beast. I found myself very much in tears watching him, even though he is not the most endearing of characters...

because it was the death of someone whose devotion to the piano was really very touching.

I'm going to go back into my studio and do some more work on this blasted "Waltz for Suzy," which I've been trying to pin down. I will press on I suppose until such time as I get a tape which seems fairly mindful of what I intend to be heard.

Meanwhile, all the best from me. Thanks again for writing.

P.S. Please excuse any gaucheness in my letter. Sam has the painful task of listening to my sometimes inadequate tapes

Letters from Dudley

July 30, 1990

Dear Peter,

I'm answering your letter as I read it and am certainly anxious that this one arrives safe and sound! I'm not sure where we are as regards to correspondence, but anyway... I have a few moments to put this down and let you know my latest news -- not that there is anything special to relate.

I came back to England and Europe to make the Tesco advertisement *[the famous series in which Dudley chases chickens across the globe]* as well as to tie up some video stuff that I had consented to do with Peter Cook.

Yes, it <u>is</u> amazing that Tesco needs any advertising! Of course, when I knew them first they were just a 'hole in the wall' grocery shop. Now they have these enormous chains of pristine and sparkling markets which are really quite dazzling in their array of stuff. One of the good things, if the only good thing that I can say about the campaign, is that all the 'free range' chickens that I advertised in the last commercial, were stripped from the Tesco shelves very quickly! I think they are trying to oust Sainsbury's from the rather superior spot they seem to have reached. Anyway, I was in Bordeaux. Didn't find any great wine there I'm afraid, although I was sitting on the hub of the industry. Anyway, it was not a bad way to go I suppose... although the life there was somewhat boring. I was getting up at all hours and driving into deserted fields to film the commercial.

When I came back to do stuff with Peter Cook, I did a sort of video 'wrap around' as they're calling it, for the video cassette version of the *Not only, but Also* shows we did in the mid- sixties. We're hoping to call it *The best of what's left of... Not only but Also.* One of the stipulations from BBC Enterprises was that we attempted to introduce it at least. We weren't sure whether it was going to work, but on viewing the material, it does seem quite charming, and we have elected to go for a particular piece of almost improvised dialogue... which I think fits the bill and the occasion quite nicely-- the subject being that we have not talked for twenty years and that we've sort of made up we're not going to talk again for another twenty years!

I <u>did</u> come over to collect my degrees from Oxford. My M.A., which was the maturation of my B.A., as well as the B.Mus. which I had left for some thirty odd years. It was a strange time, spending my days and nights in Magdalen in the President's lodging, which had seemed so far and almost unearthly when I first arrived. I did, the night of my degree ceremony, a small organ recital and a recital on the piano in the chapel, which thank God, was allowed to plummet to the depths of my early parodies. Thank God I had those up my sleeve and that it didn't seem amiss (according to the President) that I should do these things. I believe Jesus Christ has no sway in the anti-chapel, particularly at this point, so you can really be rather rude if you want to!

The Oscars came and went and I had, I suppose, one of the few occasions where I went out onto the stage not towered over by my accompanying personage-- namely Paula Abdul, the dancer... who's made quite a name for herself in videos and music. She is very tiny but is young and certainly vibrant, as well as having a body which she uses a great deal in her work. She was a sweet girl, even though I am often teased for that phrase...but she <u>was</u> --very charming and warm.

I went to Hamburg to do the series with Solti and it was two weeks of an extraordinarily concentrated time. I was playing the first movement of the Schumann Piano Concerto, part of which will be used for the video. Also, two other pieces...part of the cadenza from Tchaikovsky's B Flat Major Piano Concerto, directly after the main theme ceases... the main theme which is of course is never heard again through the duration of the movement, which made me think for a bit! I also did two variations from the Brahms Variations on a Theme of Haydn... although I gather it is not certain of course that it is Haydn's theme. Solti and I played piano together on variations #5 and #7, #5 being a rather virtuosic and hair-raising 6/8 piece, the other being that beautiful berceuse or lullaby in variation #7. I must say that the experience was really rather grand.

Solti was always a source of encouragement to me. He's 77 and full of twice the energy that I have. He is very limber and I think the main thing he suffers from is a stiffness in the neck, which is due to a calcification. He was a very wonderful person to be with, probably because he didn't insist on cramming what he felt onto me... knowing the technical requirements of an instrument. He often complained that the piano is indeed a terrible instrument to play in many ways (because he became a slave to it) and it was probably, in his view, the hardest instrument to play. I played a couple of concerts with him in Hamburg and I thought to myself as I was playing the first movement of the Schumann, "What the hell am I doing? ... This is real torture and I must be nuts!" Anyway, I did it and I suppose there is an element of achievement... I don't know!

By the way, my new film *Crazy People* will be coming over in September. We don't have a legal problem with it, there have been a lot of 'harrumphings' because of its theme and I think people have missed the point. The point being: not that we are wanting to make fun of people who are in sanitariums! -- but the age old question comes up in such circumstances... whether the incarceration of these people is really fair and where the sanity-- such as it is-- really lies?

The upshot of all this is that I really didn't see anyone. Brogan and I were doing our work in Hamburg, we had a meeting in Paris and then I had to do stuff with Peter Cook. All I could do on the days before I went was to phone my sister Barbara, who happened to be away at that time! I hope my next trip will be a little more easy. I'm coming over to do, God help me (!), another Tesco ad at the end of August and I may take a week to sort things out, such as they are, on that side of the water.

I was so pleased to read that the CD has now arrived. *[my Victorian library album]* That is wonderful news, although of course it is only a scant gesture from the world when compared to the illness of your mother. I know how you feel about the cover... I always have had a problem with those things. In fact the marketing of my material has generally always made me squirm a little. I don't know too much about it, but I feel that I do know as much as some of these people who pretend to. I know what you feel about feeling your instincts with the performance of your music, but I'm afraid that the perkiness that everyone seems to want these days is a little relentless and mindless. I think one's instincts will out in the end. It's a shame that one is not allowed always to fulfil these dreams. My disc, by the way, is being handed out to various people and to that extent... may or may not interest anyone. I don't quite know yet? My 'hypnosis tapes', as Patrick calls them. I think it's because of the comparatively slow movements of them all.

I didn't realise that you don't drive, but then again... I've never seen you at the wheel of a car, so I should have surmised. Yes, I do think there are a lot of things that one leaves until late in life. I'm not sure that I'm not leaving my piano playing too late. I'm doing a lot on my own... mainly trying to learn the 48 Preludes and Fugues, *(J.S.Bach)* which is quite a task. I don't quite know why I'm doing it or who I'm doing it for, except for myself it does give one a slightly futile feeling perhaps if this is the situation. Anyway, let's say I press on!

Fifteen minutes of music on the 'old Hollywood style'?!— *[This was my 'Suite Hollywood' for a Radio 3 programme]* it should be fun but it should be hell, I would imagine. How can the old Hollywood style be put in four instruments? Well... unless those four instruments change every other second, I can't imagine how... But I'm sure you'll find a way to fit the bill. I do know what you feel about the library situation *[a reference to 'Library' music being uncredited]*. I remember letting a couple of my tunes go for that reason, and it doesn't in fact, add an iota of reputation. It's a very questionable business. I don't think you're piling on the angst, by the way... I think it's perfectly normal to feel aggravated by being somehow denied access to a potential growth.

Yes, it is sad to hear about Margaret Lockwood's death. It's hard to believe that that gracious and wicked lady *[her famous film role]* has been and has gone. Yes, it is strange how people are going these days. The people you mentioned are all people I knew and loved of course.... there's not much space between us! 'Gert and Daisy'... what a wonderful team they were and what fun to listen to. How sad that Elsie Waters *[Gert's real name]* has gone.

Well, I guess that's it for me. I have no other news that is good, it seems! Just news that keeps coming on like the sea... inexorably, relentlessly and without too much change. So, I hope I'll catch up with you next time. I send you all good wishes.

All the best. Hope this letter gets to you! Let me know!

[signature]

P. S. There is no video of "Spring Parade" but I am going to try and get a 16mm film version of it – and transfer it to tape – which you and I will hoard disgracefully for ourselves!

October 5, 1990

Dear Peter,

Many thanks for your letter which I received the other day-- I don't know why they take so long to get to me. Anyway, it may be part of this desperate plot that the Folkestone postmen are perpetrating.

Your CD arrived and I leapt into it with great enthusiasm. What I've heard so far is delightful. It does sound as if you worked with a small orchestra, but got some terrific effects, if I may be so bold. They were excellent orchestrations, it seemed to me... and ones that made use of all of the orchestral possibilities. I will have something more to say I'm sure, when I have heard them all.

It looks as if the film of *Piano Player* is down the tubes again. It doesn't seem possible to get people interested. I can imagine why. It's not exactly a commercial film and I have a feeling that the writing is a bit too on the nose for everyone... including myself!

Yes, I only did the first movement of the Schumann *[Piano Concerto]*. I must say that it was quite a strain learning it all, but I suppose it was worthwhile. Although, one is terribly exposed in the work... often playing against single instrumental lines. *[This was for the Solti television series, "Orchestra!"]*

I think my mother's promptings on getting my B.Mus. were fairly hot and consistent, but it didn't occur to me to get the darn thing until fairly recently. By the way, I think she didn't spend any money because she didn't want to be hit over the head by people who thought she earned a lot...and therefore was going out in new clothes!

It's funny how the movie *Spring Parade* is becoming an obsession. I know how it feels. I think I was influenced by Korda's *1001 Nights* when I was a kid, rather than another film which I thought it was (but I'll be damned if I can remember what it was). I think I was rather haunted by the mythological sequences... flying horses, goddesses with many arms, etc.! I seem to remember with great clarity "My own" and "Pretty as a Picture." In fact those tunes came bustling back into my head as soon as I read your remarks about them. I remember my sister bashing through those songs. I think she felt as if she was a sort of miniature Deanna Durbin, being 'gawky' herself. "Can't help singing"-- yes I remember that one. I also remember Barbara chortling away until Deanna Durbin could have been thrust down her throat with no problem at all! However, I did like the tunes very much.

God, I wish I had seen the *[Folkestone]* air display that you mention. I really regret having left the United Kingdom at a time when all this stuff was going on. I could kick myself when I think of all the stuff that was put on especially for the Blitz, which is probably never going to happen again. Damn... it sounds so wonderful. *[The Folkestone air show was commemorating 50 years since the 'Battle of Britain' in the skies over Kent.]*

God, Athene Seyler dead. That is a strange thought. Stranger because I thought she had died some years ago! --reminds me of the old John Gielgud story, (yawn, maybe I've already told you?)-- complaining about how old actresses went on and on. He was talking to Athene Seyler, saying "All these actresses, they seem to go on and on...Sybil Thorndike, Flora Robson, Athene Seyler ... Oh, not YOU Athene!" It's fun if you've heard it for the first time!

You were very sweet in giving me your feelings about *Crazy People*. I thought it was alright to get involved with a girl who had been somewhat beaten down by life, since I wasn't going to do *Sketchlife*. Interesting, your point about our teams of writers. It was in fact written by the one guy who wrote *Good Morning Vietnam,* namely Mitch Markowitz. Unfortunately, the brevities of the cinema public's fascination were probably catered to in the case of the length of footage dedicated to my adjustment in the sanitarium. Things tend to leap around for no good reason except for reasons of time and pace, according to one 'informed mind!' I didn't write the music, because I think it would have been rather hard to do a comedy. I'm very appalled by the thought of doing comedies. They are very hard to deal with musically, I think. I much prefer the romantic, straightforward stuff of *Six Weeks.*

Thanks for your good wishes. I wish there was something I could say that would ease the burden of your life progression at this moment, but I don't suppose there is much I can do or say that will be of any real consolation. *[My Mother, whom I was nursing, was very ill at the time.]*

I wish you all good things as usual.

Letters from Dudley

December 5, 1990

Dear Peter,

Many thanks for your letter of 20th October. I just got to it, because I was in the U.K. as you might have surmised -- for the last three weeks and came running back here to do various odd things.

Thank you for your delightful remarks regarding myself and Keith Clark. Where the hell is he now? *[Keith was Dudley's contemporary at school and another brilliant pianist.]* However, I must say reading an article on Hans Von Bulow, I find my own achievements and those of most people very sparse. He seemed to have the most extraordinary memory and was able to not only play works by heart, but lesser compositions by people including chamber music and orchestral scores.

This is of course while we struggle on with our memories fading fast! I think I developed a memory only because I elected to go a little more slowly at my playing. Doing that allows one the luxury of finding things committed to memory or almost without doing too much in terms of effort.

Whilst in England, I did a Wogan show and a little advertising generally for the re-issue of some *Not Only, but Also* programmes, which Peter and I put together over the last God knows how many years. I was also doing a bit of repair work for the Solti series and of course filming strange adverts for Tesco. (I seem to have landed in a British farmyard and found myself in the middle of a Stilton enterprise.) *[still looking for the chickens]*.

Yes, I think I am mixing up the Korda *Thief of Baghdad* and the Universal 1942 film *Arabian Nights.* You seem to remember every detail of the Korda film, including all of the characters. God, it did seem to influence me enormously. Nursery psychology was very much in play at the time!

By the way, did you ever read a book by Bruno Bettelheim about the influences and reasons for the appearance of nursery rhymes and tales? Psychologically it's a fascinating book. I think it's called *The Magic of Childhood* or something like that.

I'm going to cut this letter short, since I have got to catch up with a lot of correspondence which has accumulated, as well as doing lots of trivial things...one being looking for old photographs for a film festival in the wine country above San Francisco, where they're going to be honouring me! I'm looking for one damn photograph of me as a youth, pouting slightly. It was taken at school when I was about 10.

I agree with you about *[Leonard]* Bernstein. He was an acquaintance of mine and someone I entertained with my Colonel Bogey piano sonata on several occasions. I don't think I could really take to his manner, either. I must say that seeing him conduct in L.A. was really a rather disturbing experience. All he seemed to do was jump, especially in the Tchaikovsky symphony, which he conducted at an immensely slow rate.

I agree that *West Side Story* is a classic, but I don't really like much of it except perhaps the more athletic elements. The sentimental side of it seemed to push too much in that direction.

By the way, I don't read papers that print personal stuff about me. It's generally inaccurate and hurtful. Thanks just the same, but I'll pass on receiving this stuff, since I will obviously take a lifetime to get over it!

Many thanks for your notes on 'Spring Parade.' * We will still keep an eye out for it.

Meanwhile, all the best as always,

Dudley

* Now we hear from the horse's mouth that no videos at all were made of D. Durbin! A likely story. Well, we'll keep looking & pressing & bet we turn up trumps one day!

[Luckily in 2005, for the first time, all of Deanna's films are on video and DVD, except for the elusive 'Spring Parade.']

January 30, 1992

Dear Peter,

Thanks so much for phoning Suzy's when I was in London. *[Suzy Kendall was Dudley's first wife and great friend.]* I'm sorry that I haven't been at all regular in getting back to you. I'm afraid there's no excuse except for what amounts to a really nutty schedule. In fact, things have become so nutty, that I discovered your letter among some correspondence that I took with me to London hoping to answer it, which I didn't... being run ragged by two weeks of publicity that never seemed to stop! So now I'm writing you from a New York hotel room!

Your Mother doesn't sound as if she is too well. I trust that things will be alright for you. With her turning ninety, obviously there is a lot to do to look after her and I'm sorry that you are in a state where you have to do so, to the detriment of yourself. However, I was pleased to hear that there was some movement on the music front. It does seem to be an extraordinarily long time getting things going and there is no doubt that you have been waiting far too long.

I hope I didn't offend you by asking if you had any pupils. I couldn't remember if you were teaching part time. I think you were, but what with everything else... I'm sure there isn't a moment to spare. Your life and mine are very different it seems. I am dashing around to various countries doing not much, although I'm practicing endlessly to try and get this Mozart *[Piano Concerto No. 21, K467]* and Gershwin *['Rhapsody in Blue']* in trim. I know that it's very difficult for you to get away in the evenings with your mother in this situation... but I hope that at some point you can perhaps get away. I'm sure we will talk about that in days to come.

Thanks for sending the *[Christmas]* circular... or whatever they call it over here? It was good to hear your news. In many ways, I think that the employment of such a device is the only way to get around writing to everyone. It's a way of letting everyone know what one is up to and is probably the only thing to do.

Look forward to seeing you sometime very soon,

All the best,

[The very last time I was to see Dudley, although I did not know it then, came about as the letters neared their end. He was in England.

I met him at the BBC. I can't think what I was doing there but as I came down the stairs, I heard whispers,

"It's Dudley Moore!" He was standing in the huge foyer of Broadcasting House, which for once was completely empty. For some reason he looked very vulnerable and alone. We greeted each other and went through the huge art deco doors. I was reminded of his stature as I had when he was a boy; he barely came up to my shoulder. He took me for afternoon tea at the Langham Hotel which was just across the road. The hotel had made a tea room very much in the Thirties style and a pianist tinkled away at a white piano. We were presented with a tray of delicate fondant cakes and Dudley hesitated which to choose. "I was always taught to take the one nearest to me," I said primly! I just wish I could remember all the things we talked about on that occasion. We parted on Lower Regent Street. It was the last time I was to see him in this life. I wish I had known that.]

October 27, 1992

Dear Peter,

Many thanks for your letter and tape, which I listened to immediately. *[This was a cassette of my Suite Hollywood music.]* The tape was, as always, splendid... with some wonderful haunting and beautifully sentimental phrases, which I loved very much. Thank you <u>so</u> much for letting me hear it.

I shall be coming to London 8th November for about a month. I'm busy most of the time but I hope we will at least be able to say hello. We both seem to be busy in our individual ways. Whenever I come to U.K. I seem to be doing commercials, all this stuff with Initial Television, (which I shall be doing again this time). You-- on the other hand-- are endlessly caught up with things regarding your mother. I do quite understand and can certainly believe all that you have to do. It's a very hard life and I think you are coping magnificently. It was lovely to see you, even if briefly.

I ended up by not going to Australia, for which I was sort of grateful... since the non-stop trip would have taken something like 18 hours-- a bit much in my condition, I can tell you! The commercial for Tesco was done in Los Angeles in an area which looked purportedly rather like Australia. An Aborigine chap was imported from Australia and we filmed the whole thing at a place called Malibu Creek!

I'm coming over to do what seems to be the final round in all this Tesco'ing. I <u>finally</u> find the chickens and get near them, then decide that I have to release them! It's quite a nice idea I feel. Don't tell this idea to anyone, or it will spread, I'm afraid, a little like wildfire... and I will be blamed for letting the cat out of the bag.

In any case, although I'm over for a bit of work, I hope I'll be able to see you. Yet, the prospect of getting together seems fairly remote on both sides.

I think by the way, that Max Steiner would have been very pleased with your efforts. *[He was the Warner Brothers leading film composer of the 'Golden Age.']* I hear that you did not use a huge orchestra, but I thought that the use of these five instruments was wonderful. I hope the pastoral thoughts business happens... since, I for one would be very interested to hear the result. I know that it might cause problems from a domestic point of view... but it would certainly be an eye-opener for all of us. *[This did eventually become my CD, 'A Country Calendar'.]*

I agree with your postscript, regarding the TV-AM interview; where I said that everyone needs something visual before they can appreciate classical music. I certainly did not mean that in entirety by any means, since my own appreciation of classical music was through the <u>radio</u>! I just felt that the video side of things could <u>help</u> someone to appreciate classical music. I do agree that a composer's biography is only useful for your understanding, if it actually <u>affects</u> the music you are hearing. I have found it practically impossible to absorb any details of anyone's biography, since it seems to be appallingly boring to know about someone's life. I agree that music should not have a visual stimulus, although there are some very well-known cases in my situation where actually seeing the music performed made a difference.* The one thing that is fairly visual and musical at the same time is one area where I do not really have any interest at all... and that is opera. I find it very difficult to get to grips with it.

Hope all is reasonably well with you. I say 'reasonably,' because it doesn't seem to get beyond that penn'orth of reason that we all seem to discuss daily.

Anyway...do hope to talk to you soon. Best wishes as always,

When I saw the Juilliard Stg 4tet play the Bartok Stg Qtets in Edinburgh round '57 or '59 I was very impressed by the feeling of the music but only when I saw it performed! I don't know what that means!

[The following letter is Dudley's response to the death of my Mother. She had become desperately ill, longed for her life to be over and needed 24-hour nursing. But I was able to keep her at home until her last two days and sat with her in hospital until the end. She had almost reached ninety two years. It is strange that the two shortest letters in the set are when Dudley speaks of his own Mother's death and when he reacts to the news of mine.]

May 21, 1993

Dear Peter,

I will have spoken to you by the time you get this.

I was much moved by your letter and by the tale of your mother. It was a <u>very</u> moving time. I will talk to you no doubt again about all of this.

All the best,

Dudley

P.S. I am enclosing an 8 X 10 made out to Sarah, whom you mentioned in one of your letters.

Letters from Dudley

[Sarah Daniel, my wonderful home-help, was one of Dudley's fans. She started working for us in the last six months of my Mother's life, and had a great affection for her. In Dudley's picture, he writes across it, his thanks 'for looking after Peter's mother.']

જી∘જી

February 9, 1994

Dear Peter,

Thanks for your letter of 4th December and your good wishes for the holiday and the New Year. May I wish you the same!

Glad you enjoyed the "Concerto!" series. I suspect that you've probably liked Tilson-Thomas more than Solti because he is American and understands the language perfectly. I also wasn't under the added burden of talking about things --which I knew very well and which were very easy to comment upon. Glad you approved of the full account of the works at the end—although, I must say that I agree with you regarding the lighting. I certainly don't like the way it changes with the emotional quality of the music. I don't find a strong enough reason to object to it however, but in the next series (which will probably be an ad hoc series), there will be (maybe) a different approach. I don't know ... Certainly, for the players... it is difficult in the sense that it has all been previously recorded. In another

152

sense, it isn't so difficult. I guess there are points to be said for both. *[The musicians had to mime to a playback.]*

Sorry to hear that the house is so lonely with your mother passing on. I can quite understand it, having rattled around this house-- very lonely and isolated. *[He had by now parted from Brogan.]*

I must say that I think the Lake District is the most beautiful place in the world. I was almost brought to my knees with tears when I journeyed on the road to Keswick... and there were sheets of rain coming down. It was the most beautiful sight to behold.

Hope that the radio programme, "Suite Hollywood," has been transmitted. How did it go? I'm glad that the research into your past has yielded such fascinating details. I think that our heritage too came from smugglers of the 19th Century. There my grandfather ended his search apparently! *[I researched my family history for Piers Plowright's radio programme about my grandmother, 'The Road from Marriage Farm'. It became part of the script.]*

I am probably coming to England on May 10th, for a film which I will be shooting for two months in England and France. I shall play a pugilist's agent. The film will be called *The Guv'nor*—the Guv'nor not being me, but someone you can bash into small pieces with bare hands—highly illegal-- but can be bet on. Apparently this sort of thing goes on in recent years, but I'm not aware of it. Perhaps I should be!

I'm also doing-- for the third time-- a television sitcom idea, which will be filmed sometime probably before I go. Then we shall get word whether we continue sometime in June or July. I have a feeling it will go because of politics. Not that it is my best work, but ... *[Neither of these projects happened.]*

I'm also doing concerts around the U.S., although this month doesn't see any. I shall be going to Canada and Texas before I come to England, playing my <u>tiny(!)</u> repertoire of Mozart's 21st Piano Concerto (with the "Elvira Madigan" slow movement) and the "Rhapsody in Blue," plus parodies which I've done, as you know, forever!

So, at this point, things are OK. Although I wasn't touched by the earthquake this time, who knows what horrors are in store. Apparently a size 8.0 quake in Los Angeles is not too likely,   (-one never knows!)

I hope I'll be able to talk to you when I'm in town.

Meanwhile all the best,

[At last a set of Deanna Durbin's films appeared on Video in the USA. It contained three of her youthful films, including '100 Men and a Girl' which she made with Leopold Stokowski and his orchestra, and 'It started with Eve', the best one from her later days. Dudley very kindly sent the set over to me.]

May 3, 1994

Dear Peter,

I hope you received the tapes of Deanna Durbin. I was very shocked and surprised, as well as gratified to know that some tapes were coming out. I must say, I was feeling a bit frustrated about ever seeing a Deanna Durbin film again. Apparently there is an American television channel called AMC (American Movie Channel) which does show lots of the old films.

Thank you for your thoughts about the earthquakes. It seems that I was at the corner of the activity, so wasn't really in the middle of it all. The aftershocks have also been slight in the loosening of this house. It was built to minimise the shock, but we haven't had a really bad shock in my area yet. So I have that to look forward to!

The repertoire for my concert tour is being extended in September, with the Grieg Piano Concerto! I don't recall Keith Clarke doing the first movement in those DCH *[Dagenham County High School]* concerts, almost forty years ago, however I do remember <u>him</u>! I shall be doing other lollipops: Brahms and Rachmaninoff.

The Guv'nor doesn't seem to be totally financed right now, so I've had to give it up unfortunately. I played the agent of one of those bare knucklers. It would all be fairly grim reality, as far as I know. I don't know if my comedic days are done, but they certainly are in <u>this</u> film.

The CBS television sitcom idea we won't know about until the middle of May, if they want to continue or not. (Just heard it has been picked up --but we have to do well to continue-- like everybody else!)

By the way, Piers *[Plowright]* did send me a copy of the 50-page story of your family that you wrote in connection with the Marriage Farm music recording at Maida Vale *[studios]* on May 9-10.

I found reading it fairly <u>fascinating</u>. Great stuff! The whole thing must have brought back extraordinary memories. To see your old bedroom where you used to read "The Magnet" and later Dickens.

Yes, I did see *Shadowlands*, about the affair between C.S.Lewis and the American Joy Gresham. The man was at Magdalen when I was there, but I don't think I knew him too well.

Seems that the papers and television have been making hay of my marriage, birthday, and God knows what these last few weeks! It has been a fairly ghastly week, but is all simmering down now. I'm as intrigued as anyone else to read what goes on in the *National*

Enquirer, Star, Globe, Sun, Daily Mail ... the list is endless. I like to see people dished as much as anyone else, but I'm not going to refute people who say these things and made a meal of it. I don't want to <u>perpetuate</u> stories that go on forever and are largely fabricated. Anyway(!) ...

Hope you enjoy the tapes. I will talk to you when I get to London, which seems to be a later and later date. Maybe not until July, when I come for the Ashkenazy concert.

All the best as always,

June 16, 1994

Dear Peter,

So pleased that you received the Deanna Durbin videos. I have yet to see them, but can just imagine you sitting with your gas mask watching her at the Lowestoft Odeon! *[Cinemas were closed in the first week of the Second War, but were opened again a week later and we could see Deanna in 'Three Smart Girls Grow Up', one of the delightful movies in Dudley's set.]*

Yes, it is a shame that the film *[The Guv'nor]* fell through and is also a shame that I was supposed to be doing a concert in July with Vladimir Ashkenazy in the UK which fell through as well! All eight concerts were cancelled. Whether this is an economic recession or due to recent publicity about me, I don't know. Frankly, I don't really care! If people wish to read this stuff in the tabloids and believe it, then that's their problem.

Also, BBC-II is reigning in its resources, because the concert in Carnegie Hall doesn't seem to be up for televisualization either. So... work in the UK seems to be crumbling around my ears.

Glad you were able to see the old school photographs. Yes, I myself have a copy of the one with me as a prefect next to Roy Allen. I have a feeling that was the time I was bashed up (and rattled my head against a telegraph pole!) by a spiv who thought quite rightly that I was sniggering about his girlfriend. I think that the black eye was fairly visible. I remember telling my mother that I had fallen off a chair!

Sorry you're having such awful weather—"Can't Help Singing." Yes, I remember my sister doing that at the piano, which didn't endear me to the song then. However, I'm certainly enjoying it now.

Hope to see you soon, despite all these cancellations!

Letters from Dudley

September 23, 1994

Dear Peter,

I'm not sure if you replied to my last letter or not, but thanks anyway!

The Ashkenazy concert seems to have been cancelled for no good reason, but I think it's lack of funds, which is the prime reason. I also think that impresarios are to blame for the high prices which they charge, so what's new!?

I'm glad you saw my album with the young cancer victim—Amanda Thompson. That was certainly one of my fleeting visits to the U.K.

Glad to hear that the reunion of the Goldsmiths students was OK, but one of the strangest experiences which you ever had. I wish my reunions at Dagenham had been equally impressive, but they weren't.

Hope this will find you well. I'm just on my way to New York for a Carnegie Hall benefit *[for Music For All Seasons]*, in which I'll be playing the Grieg Piano Concerto and my God-knows-how-many-playings of the Beethoven Triple Concerto, which this time will be performed with the English Steven Isserlis and Joshua Bell. *[Dudley was President of this Charity, founded by his close friends Rena Fruchter and her husband Brian Dallow.]*

So-in some haste, I bid you farewell...

December 21, 1994

Dear Peter,

Thank you so much for your Christmas 'round robin' and added note to me. I'm glad you made contact with Deanna Durbin... That sounds wonderful. *[She lives in Paris and I sent her a couple of my tapes and told her the musical influence her films had upon me as a youth. I had the privilege of a couple of letters in reply.]*

I myself, have been doing very little it seems...except waiting and wondering-- whether my TV series will be picked up again here. I think it is unlikely and it certainly would be unwelcome... since it was the most hard thing I have ever done in my life! I nearly died. The scripts to it were very good, and so I have no complaints in that way... but they stopped putting it out after three weeks and they have about nine to ten episodes to show (or not!) next season!

Concerts are not starting until February, when I shall be doing a few in the U.S. I'm enjoying more and more just playing the piano. Currently I'm playing, as you know, the Mozart K.467, "Rhapsody in Blue," and the Grieg Piano Concerto, which had the misfortune to slip under my fingers it seems!

Not much more to tell. I too wish you the best for the New Year.

[In the difficult period that began in the mid-1990s, Dudley was for the time, to turn his back on so many of his old friends. As the illness Progressive Supranuclear Palsy took hold of him, our correspondence came to an end. The few letters that I wrote remained unanswered as he went into this troubled time. On one occasion I wrote to an address in London where he was virtually in hiding, trying to get away from his turbulent fourth marriage. I felt such a great sadness for all of this.

However, towards the end of the Nineties, there was to be one final exchange between Dudley and myself. The degenerative illness had now taken hold. He still knew all the music in his mind but his fingers could no longer perform it. He said bitterly that he had become a complete caricature of himself. But he had managed to extricate himself from his disastrous marriage and a great friend, the concert pianist Rena Fruchter, was to take him into her family and in a wonderful way, to care for him during the last years of his life. In this way he found a happiness that had been hard to seek. She was later to write her own wonderful book about this last decade in Dudley's life— "Dudley Moore—An Intimate Portrait."

In my own life, with the help of my good friend Piers Plowright, now retired from the BBC, I produced two CDs. One was a Musical set in the Kentish Downland countryside in wartime, 'The Wartime Picnics'; the other, 'A County Calendar,' described in my words and music how English life used to be in the Thirties and Forties. I sent copies to Dudley, hoping he might enjoy this nostalgic account of the past. I had a reply from Rena. Dudley could no longer write but he was so glad to have them and sent his thanks and constant good wishes. He would also like me to have an enclosed CD of his work, "Live from an Aircraft Hangar." Despite his illness, he had produced and edited this from his performances. It included so many of his finest things, "Die Flabbergast," heard so many years ago at my London party, and the tremendously moving music from 'Six Weeks.'

In those last days, I was to take part in four television documentaries about Dudley, talking of early times. The best was a programme about his most overlooked gift, his fine ability as a composer. As a great surprise for Dudley, they got hold of a copy of his String Quartet, written for his BMus Oxford degree, and a quartet of four young musicians played it on the beach at Rena and Brian's summer home in Nova Scotia. Dudley was brought to this delightful scene.

Letters from Dudley

In all this account of our correspondence, it has of course, been impossible to quote from my own letters to Dudley. The very last time I was to write to him, occurred just before the Christmas of 2001. Dudley had been awarded the CBE in the Queen's Birthday Honours List. Despite being desperately ill, he came to England to receive the award in Buckingham Palace. I wrote to send him my heartiest congratulations and remember saying how proud, amazed and delighted his mother would have been. I told him how privileged I had been to have him as one of my first pupils. But an even greater privilege had been to have him as a friend. A few months later, 27th March 2002, his life was to come to an end.

There is just one of my letters of which I kept a copy and with which I want to end this book. I was honoured to be a part of a book of birthday tributes written to Dudley by friends and colleagues for his 64th Birthday. I reprised all the things I had said, and now I think it will make a fitting climax to our long correspondence.]

Folkestone.
Kent.
England.

December 12 1998

Dear Dudley,

I am sure you know that I was one of the folk who had the privilege of being filmed in the Documentary about your life and work, which has been made for American television.

When I learned that I was to be interviewed on film, I got out all the many letters you wrote to me and read them through again. And what a wonderful collection they are. Do you realise that you began in 1980 and went on until 1994, fourteen years in which you wrote 44 times, often at great length. It amazes me that you should have written in such depth, telling me so much of your feelings and philosophy, as well as fascinating accounts of all the movies you were making, the concerts you were giving and all the Hollywood people you met, (much to my enjoyment as a frustrated film fan!) And also all the tender care and interest you had in the music I was writing, and sometimes recording, at the time. Of course our acquaintance goes back a very long way, probably as much as any of your friends.

It will soon be half a century since I first met you in 1950, as a shining sixteen-year-old, and myself as Dagenham County High School's very inexperienced and not much older, Music Teacher. But even so, that you should have written with such trust and in a completely uninhibited manner, telling so much of your thoughts about life and all the Hollywood experiences you were encountering, was an honour and one I will always treasure. These are living documents and when I'm no longer on the scene, I'm making provision, (through another good friend, Piers Plowright) that the letters will be preserved, for they tell us so much. Of course when I knew about the interview, I read them very quickly, but now it is over, I'm doing so again but at leisure, just a couple at a time, often when I rise early in the morning and have that first (very English) cup of tea. And as I go through your American life by this means, it's as if you are talking to me, so direct are they. This makes sense because you used to record your ideas on tape, often just having read the letters I sent back and it was almost as if we were making conversation. And now across the years, your voice is repeating itself, to my great pleasure.

As for the television interview, I found this a very strange experience and learned a little of what you went through in all your film-making. I felt afterwards that I had not said half of what I wanted, there was so much more of the warmth, fun and regard I wanted to bring out, but everyone seemed to be very satisfied.

I expect the bulk of all this will end up on the cutting-room floor as the Documentary will only last an hour. One thing I hope remains: I read a short extract from one of your letters. You had recently seen an old Ealing film, *A Run for your Money*, and this had reminded you so much of your roots. You spoke of trying to recreate your old home in your California mansion, imagining the trains from Chadwell Heath outside, instead of the Pacific surf. It is a very fine piece of writing and tremendously evocative.

I am so terribly sorry for the difficult time that you have been having of late. You are very much in my thoughts and I just hope that things will get happier for you. I have always wished that you might write the definitive jazz-orchestral work for the new century, a millennium 'Rhapsody in Blue.' It's presumptuous of me to say this, but I am sure that it is within you.

I look back with nostalgia at the times I spent in your company during the last fifty years: playing those duets on Mrs Nobbs's piano in Seven Kings and the many happy Dagenham concerts; meeting up at Magdalen and later Edinburgh in your *Fringe* period, when even I had a work performed at the Greyfriars Kirk; odd London visits when I returned from Australia; coming out to L.A. to do 'This is Your Life' and having the great joy of seeing your beach home with its white walls, stripped pine and cathedral-like eyries; best of all, being with you for a whole, American day.

From those early school times to what were probably our last meetings, at that severe place with the supercilious waiters, and tea with fondant cakes and a tinkling pianist at the Langham Hotel opposite Broadcasting House, it has all been a great pleasure. But of course it's your letters that so recreate the times and your personality and will always continue to do so. How good it would be to hear from you again or even to meet once more. Perhaps it will come to pass.

You might recall that I have a vast store of videos of all my favourite Hollywood movies from the Golden Age. Recently I have been playing them on long Winter evenings, I don't check my index but just have the surprise of what turns up next. It was late last night but the film about to start was none other than your *Six Weeks*. You'll remember how you sent me a tape of the score you composed and how much I liked it. In our letters I asked if you could do a re-edit to get into the story faster and make more use of your wonderful melodic composition. We wrote about this at some length. Now the film that had gone before it in my viewing and seemed somehow to link into it, was an old Betty Grable Musical, *Mother Wore Tights*, a piece with much charm despite the title. It contained a ballad which I had forgotten, so it returned like a light shining in the dark, and moved me tremendously. Of course it is very sentimental, kitsch perhaps, and you must visualise Grable in a stunning white gown with her smile over her shoulder and the gentle musicality of her voice, but I haven't been able to stop singing it ever since.

The lyrics of the song seem to capture your spirit and the pleasure you have given to millions.

On which sentimental note I'll desist!

With much affection,

Sincerely,

Peter.

Letters from Dudley

ACKNOWLEDGMENTS

There are some of my friends whom I must thank for their help in making this book. Piers Plowright for his great assistance in assembling it all; Barbara Stevens, Brian Astell, Ruth Cooper (Levine) and Sarah Daniel for providing many of the photographs and especially Rena Fruchter who has made it possible to publish the book through the company she and Dudley co-founded, Martine Avenue Productions, which can ensure that all the profits will go to the charities that were so dear to his heart—Music for All Seasons, taking the healing power of music to those confined in institutions, and the Dudley Moore Research Fund for PSP, searching for a cure for the condition that took Dudley's life on March 27, 2002.

Peter Cork

FILMOGRAPHY

1996 – A Weekend in the Country

1995 - The Disappearance of Kevin Johnson

1992 - Blame It on the Bellboy

1990 - Crazy People

1988 - Arthur 2: On the Rocks

1987 - Like Father, Like Son

1986 - The Adventures of Milo and Otis

1985 - Santa Claus

1984 - Best Defense

1984 - Micki + Maude

1984 - Unfaithfully Yours

1983 - Lovesick

1982 - Six Weeks

1981 - Arthur

1980 - Wholly Moses!

1979 - '10'

1978 - Foul Play

1978 - The Hound of the Baskervilles

1972 - Alice's Adventures in Wonderland

1969 - The Bed Sitting Room

1969 – Monte Carlo or Bust

(aka- Those Daring Young Men in Their Jaunty Jalopies]

1967 - Bedazzled

1966 – 30 is a Dangerous Age, Cynthia

1966 – The Wrong Box

Letters from Dudley

PETER CORK, EDITOR

Peter Cork first met Dudley Moore in 1950. He was then a youthful 24-year old musician who had begun his career as a composer. He met the teen-age Dudley during his first teaching post, as head of the music department of Dagenham County High School, a coeducational Grammar School in London. Peter Cork immediately recognized the extraordinary talent of his young pupil, coaching and guiding him through the remaining years of school life. Later, a lifelong friendship developed between the two, Dudley and Peter corresponding for many years.

Peter Cork was born in 1926 in Waterbeach, a village near Cambridge, England, the only child of a Baptist Minister and his wife. He was first introduced to music by his grandfather, whose enormous record collection of show music and popular music of the time inspired the young boy. His parents, recognizing his music talent, bought a piano and arranged music lessons. Later, at the end of the Second World War, Peter trained to become a music teacher, studying at Goldsmiths College. After serving in the Royal Air Force, he continued his education at the Royal College of Music, as a composition pupil of Doctor Gordon Jacob.

He remained in his first teaching post until 1962, when he had an opportunity to teach in Sydney, Australia. There, he won the New South Wales choral cup with his boys' choir. He liked Australian life and went back for two further teaching sessions in 1965 and 1968, becoming quite nomadic, with much travel in the Far East and the Pacific, from the Angkor temples in Cambodia to Bali, Fiji and Tahiti.

When he finally returned to England in 1969, he became Head of Music at Clapham County School, a London Grammar School for girls. While there he wrote three full length period musicals-- story, libretto and music-- for the girls to perform. *The Bells of Craxminster* was set in Edwardian days, *The White Bird* in a Cornish fishing village during the Second War and *Halfway up the Mountain* during the Silver Jubilee of King George the Fifth.

Peter recalls Dudley coming to a performance of *The White Bird*, and there was much excitement among the girls at the presence of such a celebrity. A queue formed across the Great Hall during the interval, as the girls waited for his autograph. The start of the Second Act was heavily delayed!

At the age of fifty, Peter decided after 27 years to give up full-time teaching in order to compose professionally. With some guidance from Dudley, he began writing 'Library' music, more than a hundred 'Period' pieces commissioned by major music companies to be used without composer credit in film, television and radio. To his surprise, they were used in Britain and internationally. He also composed for BBC Radio, and scored documentaries produced by his friend and colleague Piers Plowright. In one of these, *The Road from Marriage Farm*, about the life of his grandmother, Peter wrote both the script and music.

In the last five years, Peter Cork has also produced two CDs of his own music. "The Wartime Picnics," is a love story set in the home-front wartime years, based around three picnics on the Kentish Downs. "A Country Calendar" tells the story, in his words and music, of country life in the Thirties and Forties.

"Through the Looking-glass," his latest CD, is an instrumental suite based on Lewis Carroll's second Alice story. This CD also includes his orchestral suite, "A Man of Kent," as recorded by the Royal Ballet Sinfonia, conducted by Gavin Sutherland. In 2005, he completed his piano suite "Country Pictures," a Piano Suite.

Peter Cork continues to compose and perform piano recitals, and takes many walking tours throughout the English countryside.

Through the Looking Glass
and
A Man of Kent
by
Peter Cork
Campion Cameo 2031

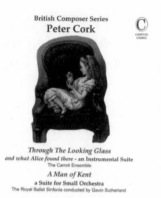

British Composer Series
Peter Cork

Through The Looking Glass
and what Alice found there - an Instrumental Suite
The Carroll Ensemble
A Man of Kent
a Suite for Small Orchestra
The Royal Ballet Sinfonia conducted by Gavin Sutherland

Through the Looking Glass
An Instrument Suite based on the Tenniel illustrations to Lewis Carroll's book, *Through the Looking-Glass* and what Alice found there.
Performed by the Carroll Ensemble conducted by Peter Cork

In the year 1933, on his sixth birthday, Peter Cork was given a present by his Mother, Lewis Carroll's Through the Looking-Glass. It became a favourite book, but he became equally fascinated and not a little frightened by the Tenniel pictures which accompanied Alice's story and her dream. Now, more than seventy years later, he has made an Instrumental Suite, mixed strings, woodwind and piano, following these macabre and imaginative illustrations.

A Man of Kent
A Suite for Small Orchestra
The Royal Ballet Sinfonia conducted by Gavin Sutherland

A Man of Kent is an evocation of the Kentish countryside south of the River Medway, hence its title (Kentish Men live to the north, Men of Kent to the south.) The three movements comprise Romney Marsh, Alkham Valley and The White Cliffs. The Romney Marsh movement has a folk-song quality, suggesting the fascination of a far and lonely distance on a clear marshland day. Alkham Valley makes use of the folk ballad, *The Lark in Still Air* creating a gentle and romantic portrait. After noisy seagulls, The White Cliffs continues with a lively maritime theme while its heroic second subject could embody the spirit of Dover in the hell-fire corner days of the Second War.

Letters from Dudley

The Wartime Picnics by Peter Cork
A love-story set in the Kentish countryside during the Second World War.

The Wartime Picnics tells a love-story in a poignant world. This 90 minute Musical evolves around three picnics on the Kentish Downs near the Pilgrim's Way, Easter Monday 1942, August Bank Holiday 1944 and Guy Fawkes Day 1946. Dramatic, tender and gently funny, the story follows an ordinary Kentish family, their life on the wartime home front and the growing love of Grace for a young airman, David. The clouds of war gather around their happiness, but the message of this evocation of 1940's Britain is ultimately optimistic. The composer lived through these times and this Musical is his testament to them.

A Country Calendar by Peter Cork
A Country Calendar describes English life as it used to be in the Nineteen Thirties, Forties and early Fifties, a time so different it could be another world. The words and instrumental music by Peter Cork evoke the countryside with scenes ranging from the Cumbrian Lakes and the Yorkshire Dales to the coastal paths of Cornwall and the Kentish Downs.

The songs and films of the time are remembered and all the special events of the year: January Snow, Valentine's Day, Mothering Sunday, Easter, Maytime and Whit Monday Fairs, the First Cuckoo, July Storms, Cockney Seaside Trips, the Battle of Britain in September Skies, Harvest Festivals, November the Fifth, Armistice Day, the magic of a frosty Christmas and New Year bells. The twelve months of the year add up to two and a half hours of nostalgic remembrance. The recording is enhanced by the great talent of the speakers, Rosemary Leach, Tim Pigott-Smith and Denis Quilley.

Both CDs were produced by Piers Plowright and the music conducted by Peter Cork All three CDs are obtainable from Campion Records (Disc Imports Ltd).
Magnus House, 8 Ashfield Road, Cheadle, Cheshire, SK8 1BB, United Kingdom.

Telephone: +44 (0)161 492 6655
Web: **www.dimusic.co.uk**

Fax: +44 (0)161 491 6658
E-mail: **dimus@aol.com**

MARTINE AVENUE PRODUCTIONS, INC.

Martine Avenue Productions was co-founded by Dudley Moore and Rena Fruchter, Dudley's musical and business partner. It was Dudley's goal for the company to present his works to the public. CDs produced by the company include "Live From an Aircraft Hangar," "Jazz Jubilee," "Jazz, Blues & Moore," and "Dudley." In addition to protecting and disseminating Dudley's work, an important part of the company's mission is donating funds to charities, including the two that were most important to Dudley—Music For All Seasons, bringing the healing power of music to those confined to residential facilities, and the Dudley Moore Research Fund for PSP, searching for a cure for the disease which took his life in March of 2002.

For additional information, please contact:
Martine Avenue Productions, Inc.
Box 221• Fanwood, NJ 07023, USA • 908 754 4190
www.dudleycd.com